THINKING KIDS™
MATH

Learning Fun for Growing Minds!

Thinking Kids™
Carson-Dellosa Publishing LLC
Greensboro, North Carolina

Thinking Kids™
Carson-Dellosa Publishing LLC
P.O. Box 35665
Greensboro, NC 27425 USA

ISBN 978-1-4838-0205-3

Table of Contents

Introduction

Welcome to *Thinking Kids™ Math!* This book contains everything you and your child need for hands-on learning and math practice. It gives you the tools to help fill knowledge gaps and build foundations that will prepare your child for higher-level math. Your child will learn to think about, know, apply, and reason with math concepts.

Thinking Kids™ Math is organized into five sections based on the skills covered. Each activity supports the Common Core State Standards and offers a fun and active approach to essential first grade math skills. Interactive lessons and the use of manipulatives build a concrete example of math concepts to help your child develop mathematical understanding.

Work through the interactive activities with your child using manipulatives around your house. Guide your child through each activity, and then allow them to perform the activity with little or no support.

Examples of common household items you could substitute for counters or blocks are different colored buttons, paper clips, pennies, and dice. A variety of manipulatives in different colors, sizes, textures, and shapes is essential to your child's learning. It is important for them to interact with different types of manipulatives so they do not associate certain concepts with certain manipulatives.

Thinking Kids™ Math promotes the use of manipulatives to engage and challenge your child. The interaction with manipulatives promotes motor skills and exploration while engaging your child in hands-on experience. Activities also call for children to draw, use tally marks, pictures, and graphic organizers. After children have worked with manipulatives, they transfer their understanding of the concept by drawing pictures in place of the manipulatives.

Each activity supports early learning standards and challenges your child's critical thinking and problem solving skills. In *Thinking Kids™ Math*, your child will learn about:

- Numbers and Operations
- Algebra
- Geometry
- Measurement
- Data Analysis and Probability

© Carson-Dellosa
CD-704462

Put the correct number of crackers on each pan. Use counters.

© Carson-Dellosa
CD-704462

Cracker Count

Put the correct number of crackers on each pan. Use counters.

Catching Fish

Look at the number. Catch that number of fish by circling the fish in the pond.

Catching Fish

Write a number. Catch that number of fish by circling the fish in the pond.

How Many Socks?

Count the socks in each row. Write the number of socks. Then, circle even or odd.

 _____ even
----
_____ odd

 _____ even
----
_____ odd

 _____ even
----
_____ odd

How Many Socks?

Count the socks in each row. Write the number of socks. Then, circle even or odd.

 _____ even
....
_____ odd

 _____ even
....
_____ odd

 _____ even
....
_____ odd

Make a chain with 23 paper clips. Separate the chains into groups of 10. Put each chain of 10 paper clips under tens. Put the leftovers under ones. Write the number of tens and ones and the total number of paper clips.

tens	ones

_____ ten(s) and _____ one(s) is _____ .

Make a chain with paper clips. Separate the chains into groups of 10. Put each chain of 10 paper clips under tens. Put the leftovers under ones. Write the number of tens and ones and the total number of paper clips.

tens	ones

_____ ten(s) and _____ one(s) is _____.

Balloon Bunches

Put a counter on each balloon. Write the number of tens and ones and the total. Draw balloons to show and write the total in the last box.

_____ ten

_____ ones

_____ total

_____ ten

_____ ones

_____ total

2 tens

4 ones

_____ total

Thinking Kids™ Math
Grade 1

Balloon Bunches

Put a counter on each balloon. Write the number of tens and ones and the total. Draw balloons to show and write the total in the last box.

_____ ten	_____ ten	2 tens
_____ ones	_____ ones	3 ones
_____ total	_____ total	_____ total

Balloon Bunches

Put a counter on each balloon. Write the number of tens and ones and the total. Draw balloons to show and write the total in the last box.

_____ ten

_____ ones

_____ total

_____ ten

_____ ones

_____ total

__2__ tens

__2__ ones

_____ total

Balloon Bunches

Put a counter on each balloon. Write the number of tens and ones and the total. Draw balloons to show and write the total in the last box.

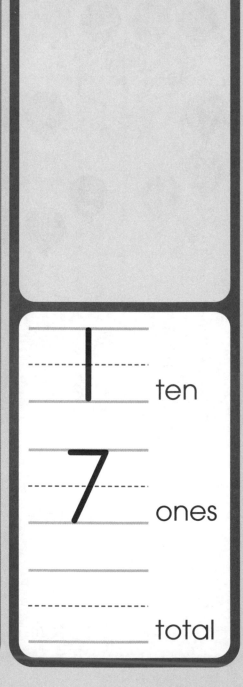

_____ ten

_____ ones

_____ total

_____ ten

_____ ones

_____ total

1 ten

7 ones

_____ total

Pinball Numbers

Write numbers to complete the chart. Use counters to help you. The first one has been done for you.

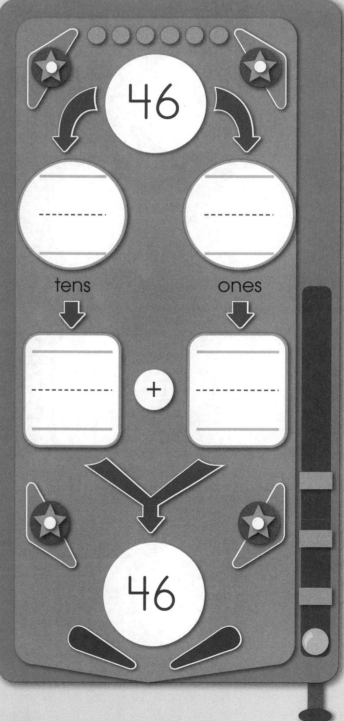

Pinball Numbers

Write numbers to complete the charts. Use counters to help you.

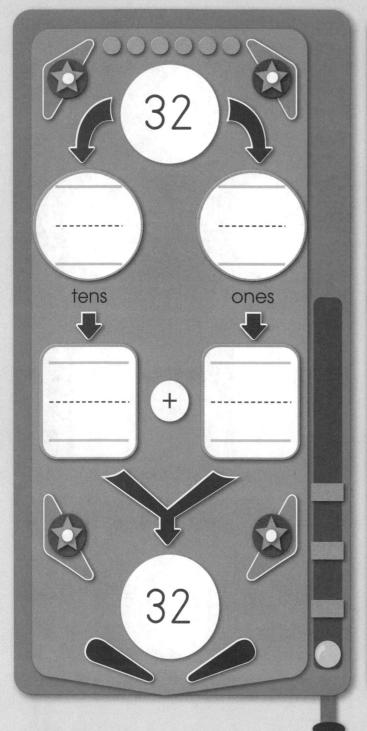

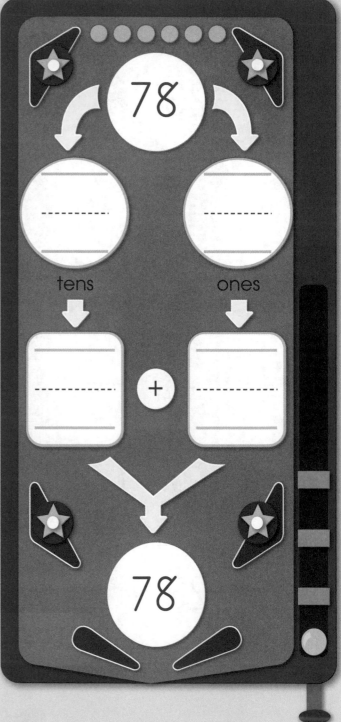

Pinball Numbers

Write numbers to complete the charts. Use counters to help you.

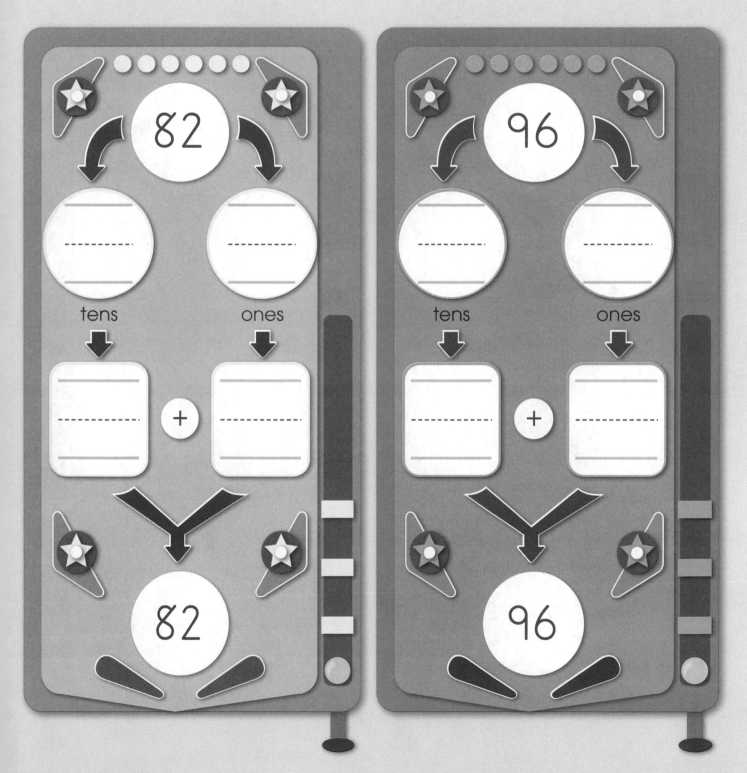

Pinball Numbers

Write numbers to complete the charts. Use counters to help you.

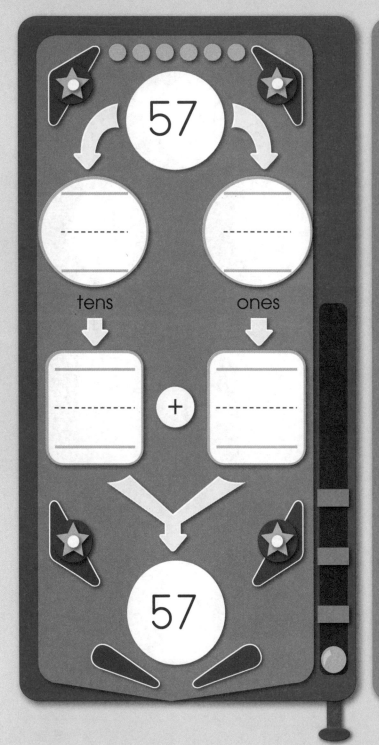

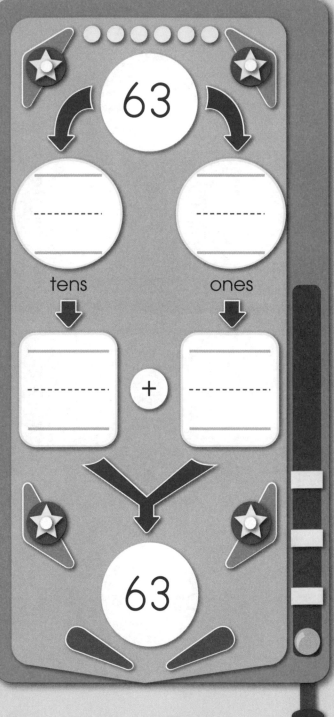

Count the peas and carrots. Circle groups of 10. Write how many tens and ones. Write the total. Then, answer the question.

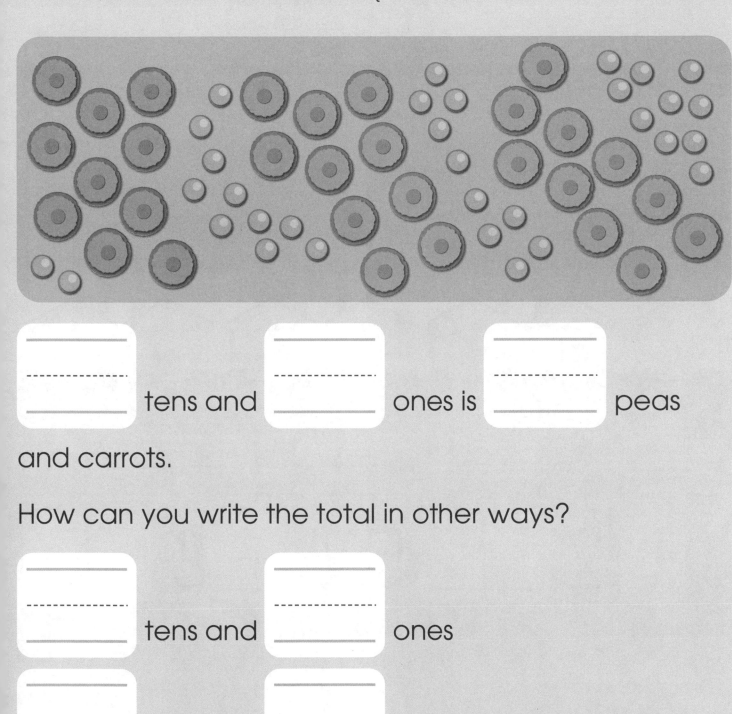

_____ tens and _____ ones is _____ peas and carrots.

How can you write the total in other ways?

_____ tens and _____ ones

_____ tens and _____ ones

Traffic Jam

Put cars on the street. Use counters. Write the missing number under each car.

- A red car is 1st.
- A blue car is 4th.

- A green car is 10th.
- A brown car is 3rd.

- A black car is 7th.
- A white car is 9th.

Put cars on the street. Use counters. Write the missing number under each car.

- An orange car is 2nd.
- A pink car is 5th.

- A purple car is 8th.
- A gray car is 6th.

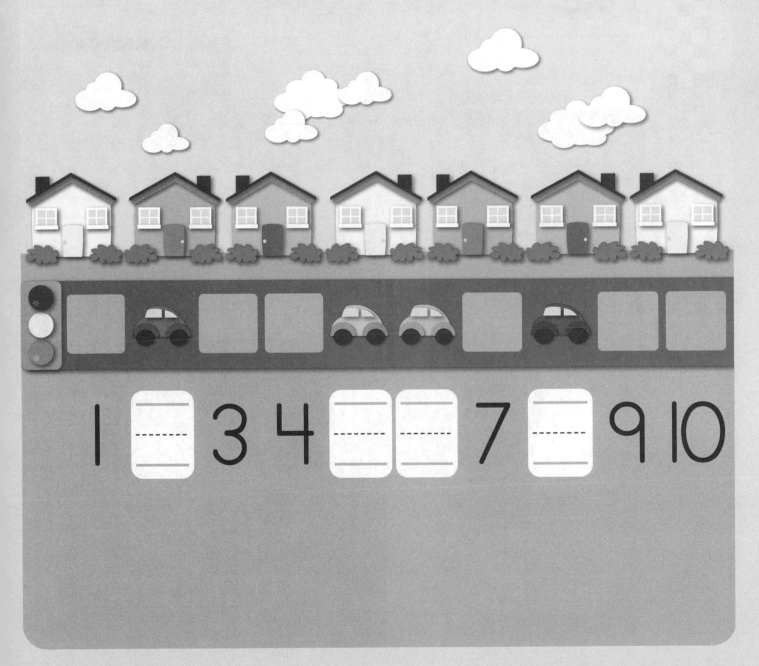

Speedy Snails

Write the number on the shell or the ordinal number word on the line to show the order the snails will finish the race.

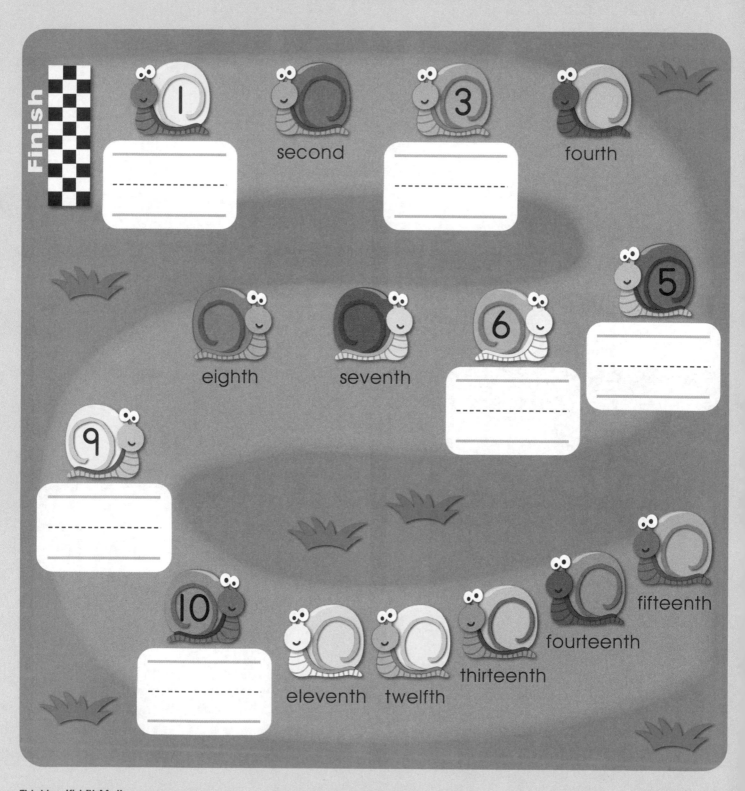

Speedy Snails

Write the number on the shell or the ordinal number word on the line to show the order the snails will finish the race.

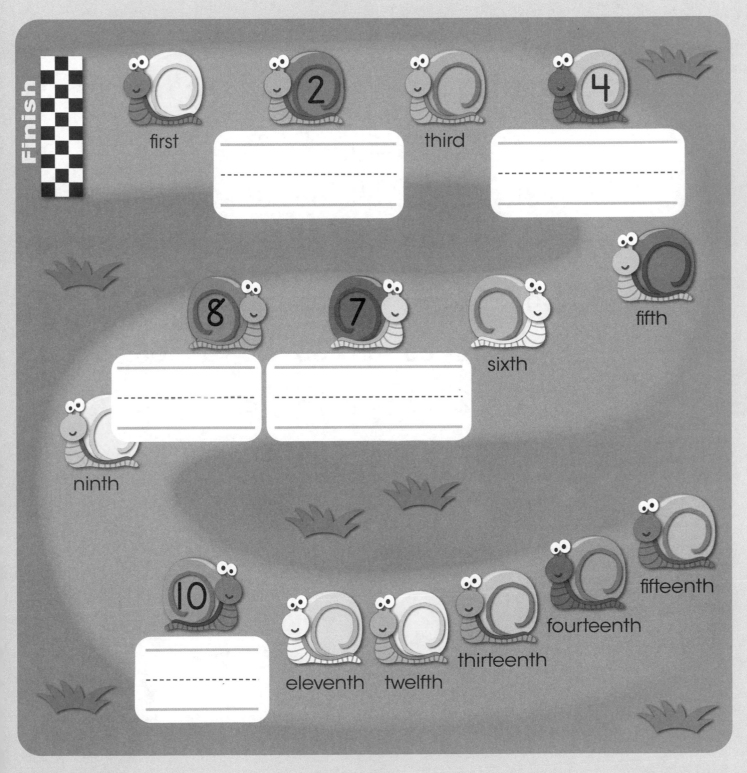

Puppy Playtime

Help the puppy count to 100. Write the number that is hidden under each object.

	1	2	3	4	5	6	7	8	9	10
	11	12	13	14	15	16	●	18	19	20
	21	22	23	24	🦴	26	27	28	29	30
	31	32	33	34	35	36	37	38	39	40
	41	42	43	44	45	46	47	48	49	50
	51	52	53	54	55	56	57	58	59	60
	🍽	62	63	64	65	66	67	68	69	70
	71	72	73	★	75	76	77	78	79	🦴
	81	82	83	84	85	86	87	88	89	90
	91	92	93	94	95	96	97	98	99	100

⚫ = _____

🦴 = _____

🍽 = _____

★ = _____

〰 = _____

Puppy Playtime

Help the puppy count to 100. Write the number that is hidden under each object.

⊙⊙⊙ = _____

1	2	3	4	5	6	7	8	9	10
11	12	⊙⊙⊙	14	15	16	17	18	19	20
21	22	23	24	25	26	🦴	28	29	30
31	32	33	34	35	36	37	38	39	40
41	42	43	🥣	45	46	47	48	49	50
51	52	53	54	55	56	57	58	59	60
61	62	63	64	65	66	67	⭐	69	70
71	72	73	74	75	76	77	78	79	80
81	Ƨ	83	84	85	86	87	88	89	90
91	92	93	94	95	96	97	98	99	100

🦴 = _____

🥣 = _____

⭐ = _____

Ƨ = _____

Thinking Kids™ Math
Grade 1

© Carson-Dellosa
CD-704462

Square Subtraction

Use the hundred board to solve each problem. Circle the first number in the problem on the board. Then, draw a path on the board as you count back to subtract the second number. Draw a triangle around the answer. Write the answer to complete the number sentence.

22 – 11 = _____   67 – 14 = _____   36 – 9 = _____

88 – 12 = _____   94 – 5 = _____   51 – 12 = _____

1	2	3	4	5	6	7	8	9	10
11	12	13	14	15	16	17	18	19	20
21	22	23	24	25	26	27	28	29	30
31	32	33	34	35	36	37	38	39	40
41	42	43	44	45	46	47	48	49	50
51	52	53	54	55	56	57	58	59	60
61	62	63	64	65	66	67	68	69	70
71	72	73	74	75	76	77	78	79	80
81	82	83	84	85	86	87	88	89	90
91	92	93	94	95	96	97	98	99	100

Shake and Spill

Put 5 counters in a cup. Shake and spill them onto the page. Write 4 number sentences describing the counters.

------------ + ------------ = ------------   ------------ + ------------ = ------------

------------ + ------------ = ------------   ------------ + ------------ = ------------

Shake and Spill

Put 10 counters in a cup. Shake and spill them onto the page. Write 4 number sentences describing the counters.

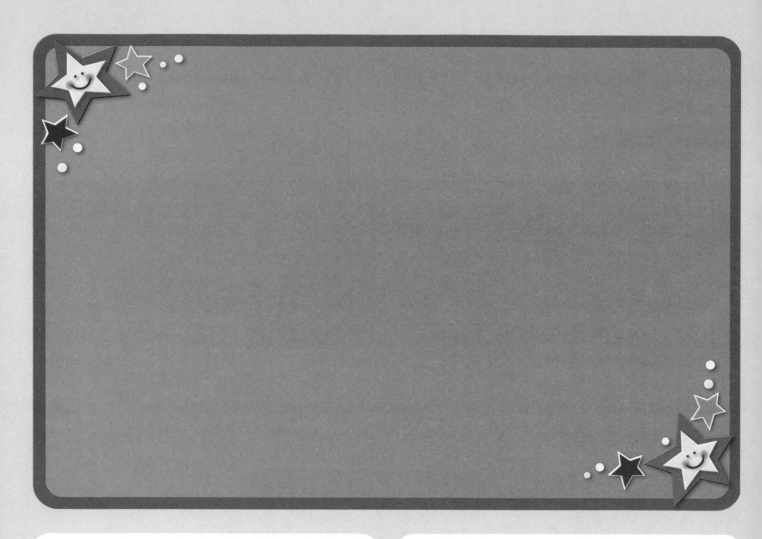

_____ + _____ = _____

_____ + _____ = _____

_____ + _____ = _____

_____ + _____ = _____

Look at the number. Put counters in the 2 flower beds to show the number. Remove the counters and draw that number of flowers.

Filling Flower Beds

Look at the number. Put counters in the 2 flower beds to show the number. Remove the counters and draw that number of flowers.

Draw a door around the number that is greater on each house.

28   82

94   49

63   36

18   81

14   41

The More Door

Draw a door around the number that is greater on each house.

51   15

24   42

43   34

90   60

87   78

The More Door

Draw a door around the number that is greater on each house.

43 34

67 76

91 19

58 85

79 97

Thinking Kids™ Math
Grade 1

The More Door

Draw a door around the number that is greater on each house.

29 92

35 53

46 64

86 68

51 15

Read each number. Circle the correct number word. Show the number in 2 different ways using pictures, number sentences, or tally marks.

5

three   seven   five

9

nine   zero   three

14

sixteen   fourteen   four

16

eleven   sixteen   twelve

Read each number. Circle the correct number word. Show the number in 2 different ways using pictures, number sentences, or tally marks.

6

four   six   seven

11

nine   zero   eleven

15

five   fifteen   four

17

eleven   sixteen   seventeen

Count the bubbles in each bathtub. Write the number on the line. Circle the correct number word.

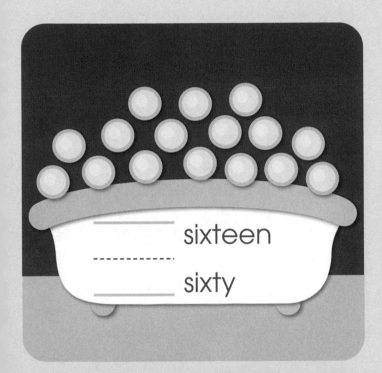

_____ sixteen

_____ sixty

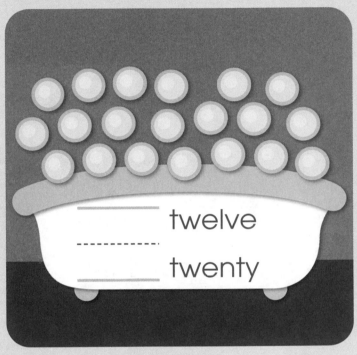

_____ twelve

_____ twenty

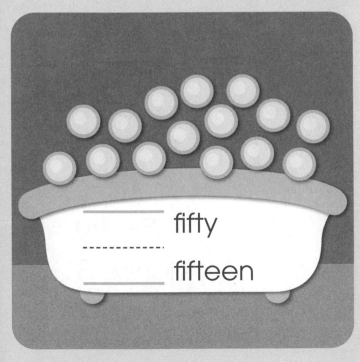

_____ fifty

_____ fifteen

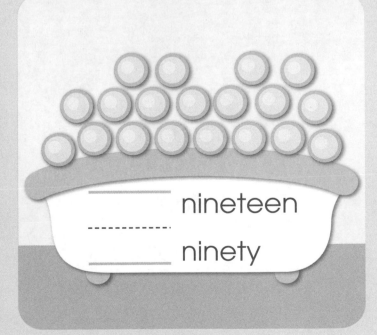

_____ nineteen

_____ ninety

Bubble Count

Count the bubbles in each bathtub. Write the number on the line. Circle the correct number word.

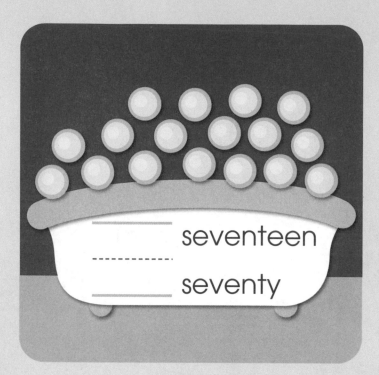

_____ seventeen

_____ seventy

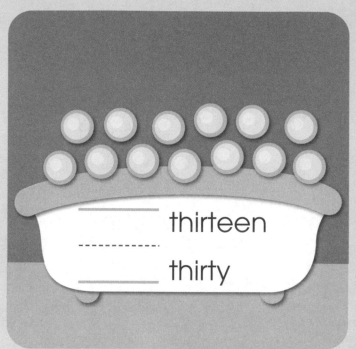

_____ thirteen

_____ thirty

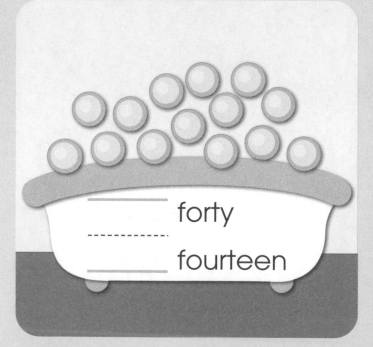

_____ forty

_____ fourteen

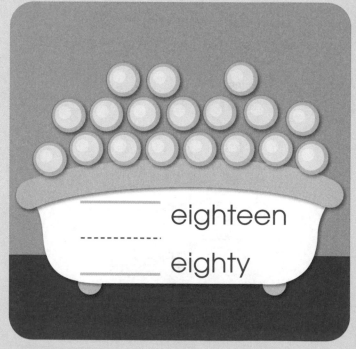

_____ eighteen

_____ eighty

By the Slice

Circle each pizza that shows equal parts.

Fraction Snacks

Draw lines to divide each snack into equal parts to show the bottom number of the fraction. Draw an X on one part to show the fraction.

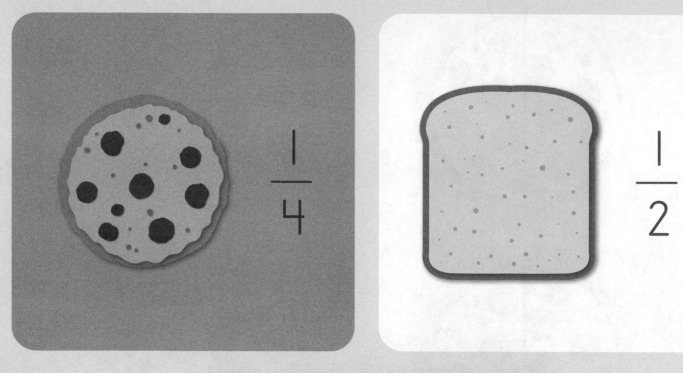

$\frac{1}{4}$

$\frac{1}{2}$

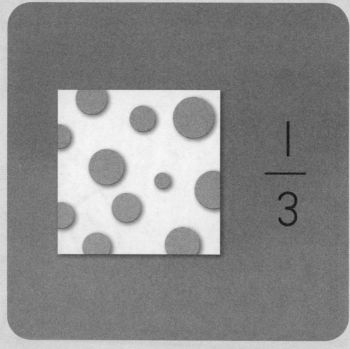

$\frac{1}{3}$

Fraction Snacks

Draw lines to divide each snack into equal parts to show the bottom number of the fraction. Draw an X on one part to show the fraction.

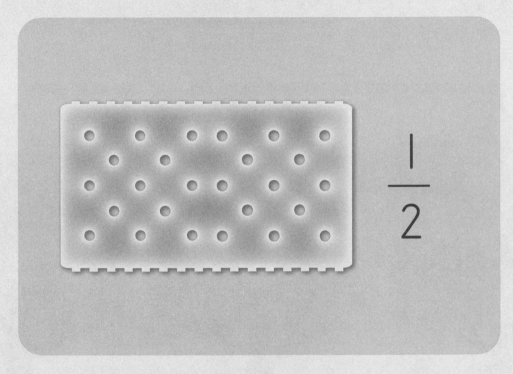

$$\frac{1}{2}$$

$$\frac{1}{4}$$

Apple Picking

Write the fractions of red and yellow apples in each tree. The first two have been started for you.

red	yellow	red	yellow	red	yellow
7	7	8	8		

Write the fractions of red and yellow apples in each tree.

red	yellow	red	yellow	red	yellow

Nest Sets

Look at the numbers below the first and second nests. Put eggs in the nests to show the numbers use counters. Move the eggs to the last nest. Write the sum.

4 + 3 = ___

Nest Sets

Write a number below the first and second nests. Put eggs in the nests to show the numbers use counters. Move the eggs to the last nest. Write the sum.

Planting On

Count the vegetables in each row. Put a counter in each box and count on to make the sum at the end of each row.

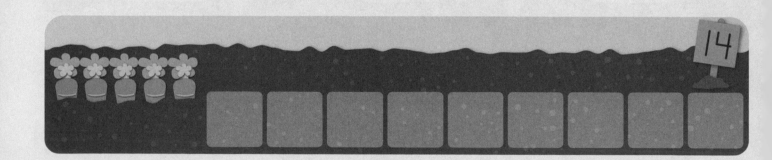

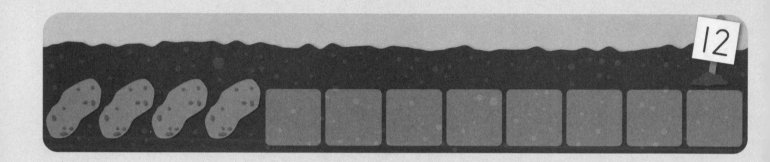

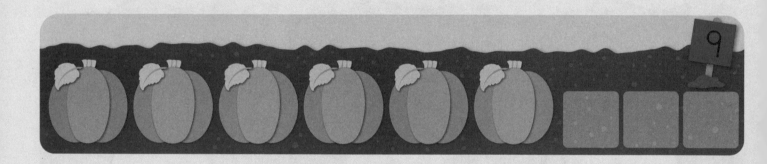

Planting On

Count the vegetables in each row. Put a counter in each box and count on to make the sum at the end of each row.

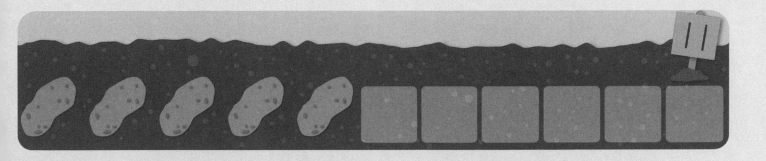

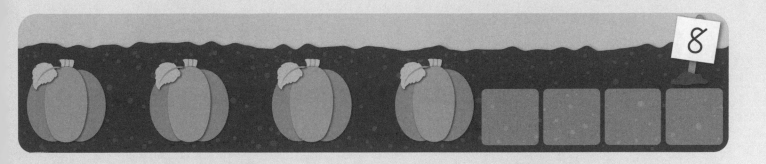

Bears' Lair

Put 8 bears in the cave. Use counters. Roll the die and subtract that many bears. Write the number sentence. Repeat three more times.

Bears' Lair

Put 10 bears in the cave. Use counters. Roll the die and subtract that many bears. Write the number sentence. Repeat three more times.

----------- − ----------- = -----------

----------- − ----------- = -----------

----------- − ----------- = -----------

----------- − ----------- = -----------

Thinking Kids™ Math
Grade 1

© Carson-Dellosa
CD-704462

Frogs on a Log

Roll a die. Starting at 10, count back the rolled number as hops on the log. Write what you did as a subtraction fact. Repeat five more times.

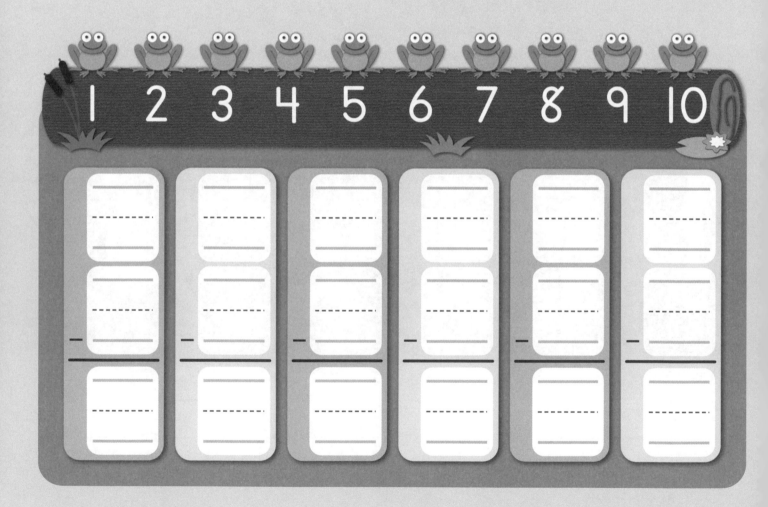

Count the gumballs in the pair of gumball machines. Write a number sentence to show how many more gumballs are in the first machine.

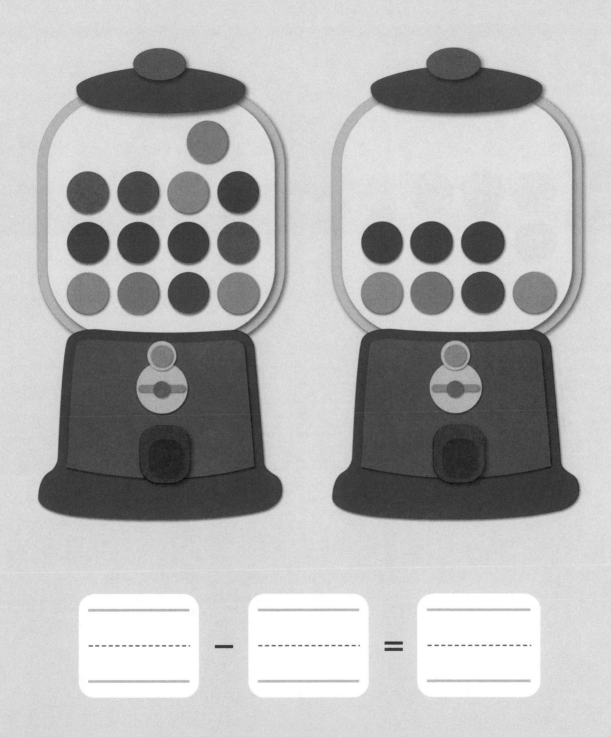

_____ − _____ = _____

How Many More?

Count the gumballs in the pair of gumball machines. Write a number sentence to show how many more gumballs are in the first machine.

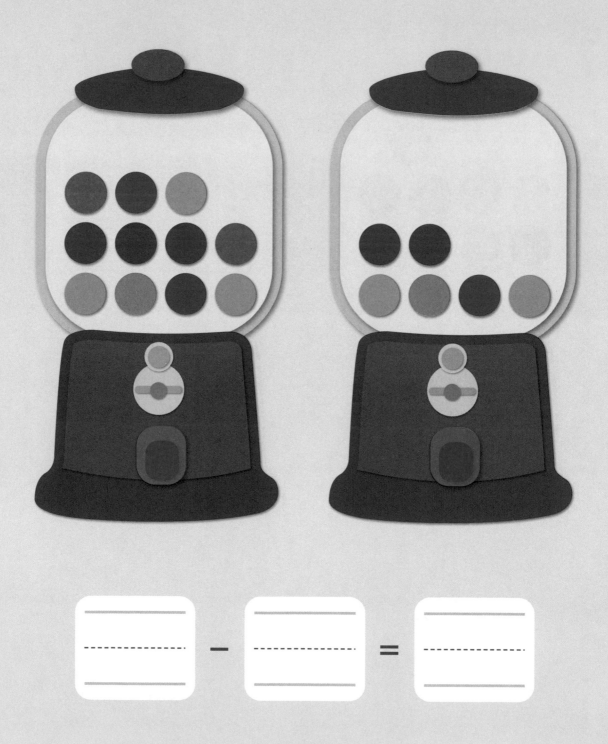

Blastoff Facts

Write the four facts for each fact family.

6, 9, 15

___ + ___ = ___

___ + ___ = ___

___ − ___ = ___

___ − ___ = ___

4, 8, 12

___ + ___ = ___

___ + ___ = ___

___ − ___ = ___

___ − ___ = ___

Thinking Kids™ Math
Grade 1

© Carson-Dellosa
CD-704462

Blastoff Facts

Write the four facts for each fact family.

6, 7, 13

___ + ___ = ___

___ + ___ = ___

___ − ___ = ___

___ − ___ = ___

8, 9, 17

___ + ___ = ___

___ + ___ = ___

___ − ___ = ___

___ − ___ = ___

Seeing Spots

Look at the domino in each box. Each domino represents a fact family. Then, write the related facts for each fact family.

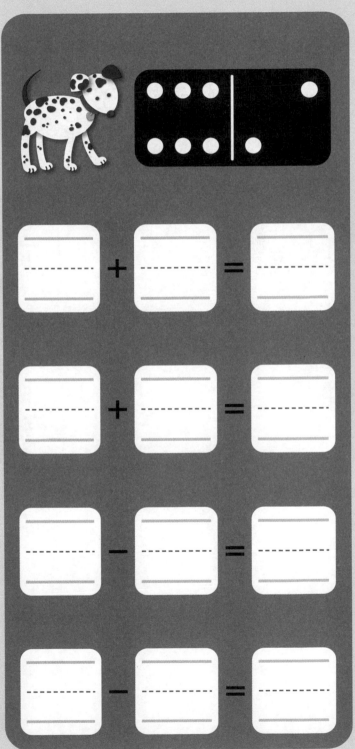

Seeing Spots

Look at the domino in each box. Each domino represents a fact family. Then, write the related facts for each fact family.

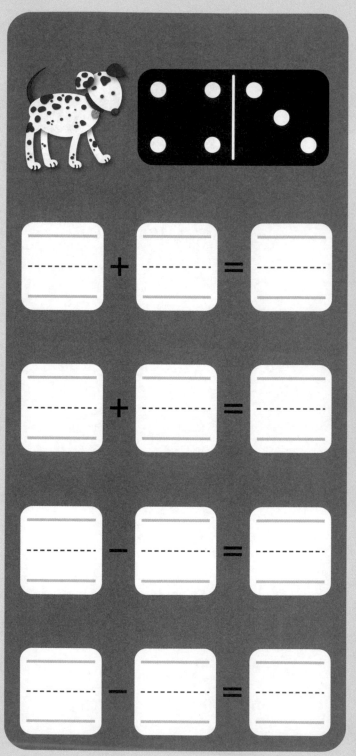

Three children picked cherries. Add the three amounts of cherries that each child picked.

Jan

+

Ruby

+

Uri

+

Baskets of Cherries

Three children picked cherries. Add the three amounts of cherries that each child picked.

Mike

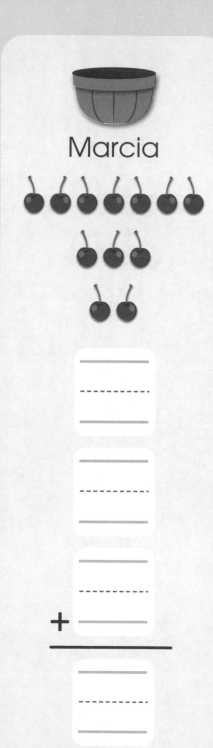

Marcia

Tom

Mystery Signs

Write + or – to make each number sentence true.

9 ◇ 5 = 14

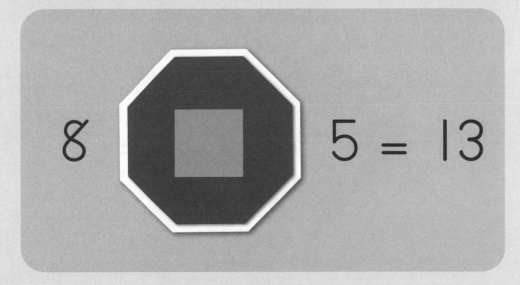

8 ⬡ 5 = 13

Mystery Signs

Write + or – to make each number sentence true.

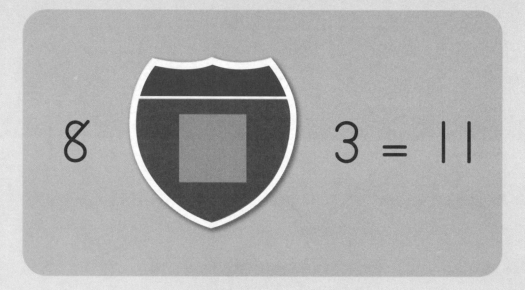

$8 \; \boxed{} \; 3 = 11$

$16 \; \boxed{} \; 9 = 7$

Put a counter on each acorn and each peanut. Divide each set of nuts into two equal groups so that the squirrels will have equal shares.

Let's Share!

Put a counter on each acorn and each peanut. Divide each set of nuts into two equal groups so that the squirrels will have equal shares.

Seeing Double

Roll a die and draw the dots in the box. Then, use the number to write a doubles fact number sentence. The first one has been done for you.

$$5 + 5 = 10$$

____ + ____ = ____

____ + ____ = ____

____ + ____ = ____

____ + ____ = ____

____ + ____ = ____

Count on to solve each problem. The common sum is the spot where the pirate buried his treasure. Mark the spot on the number line with an X.

$$10 + 8$$

$$14 + 4$$

$$16 + 2$$

$$11 + 7$$

$$9 + 9$$

$$15 + 3$$

Count on to solve each problem. The common sum is the spot where the pirate buried his treasure. Mark the spot on the number line with an X.

0 1 2 3 4 5 6 7 8 9 10 11 12 13 14 15 16 17 18 19 20

$$10 + 6$$

$$12 + 4$$

$$14 + 2$$

$$11 + 5$$

$$8 + 8$$

$$13 + 3$$

Count Back to Takeoff!

Put 20 counters on the rocket. Count back from 20 by rolling one die and removing that number of counters.

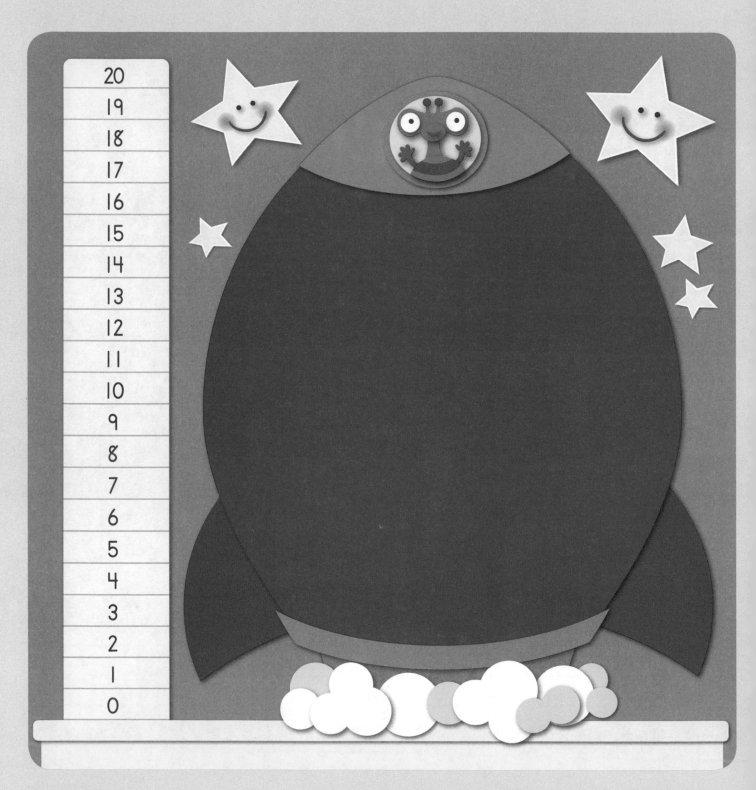

20
19
18
17
16
15
14
13
12
11
10
9
8
7
6
5
4
3
2
1
0

Flip It!

Solve each addition problem. Use the addition facts to help you solve each subtraction problem.

18 − 9 = _____ → **THINK** → 9 + _____ = 18

14 − 6 = _____ → **THINK** → 6 + _____ = 14

17 − 8 = _____ → **THINK** → 8 + _____ = 17

15 − 7 = _____ → **THINK** → 7 + _____ = 15

Thinking Kids™ Math
Grade 1

© Carson-Dellosa
CD-704462

Flip It!

Solve each addition problem. Use the addition facts to help you solve each subtraction problem.

18 − 8 = _____ → **THINK** → 8 + _____ = 18

14 − 5 = _____ → **THINK** → 5 + _____ = 14

17 − 6 = _____ → **THINK** → 6 + _____ = 17

15 − 4 = _____ → **THINK** → 4 + _____ = 15

Start with the middle number. Write the numbers that are 1 more and 2 more. Then, write the numbers that are 1 less and 2 less.

More or Less

Start with the middle number. Write the numbers that are 1 more and 2 more. Then, write the numbers that are 1 less and 2 less.

Two-Color Sums

Use two different colors of counters to make each row. Then, write two addition facts that show the color amounts.

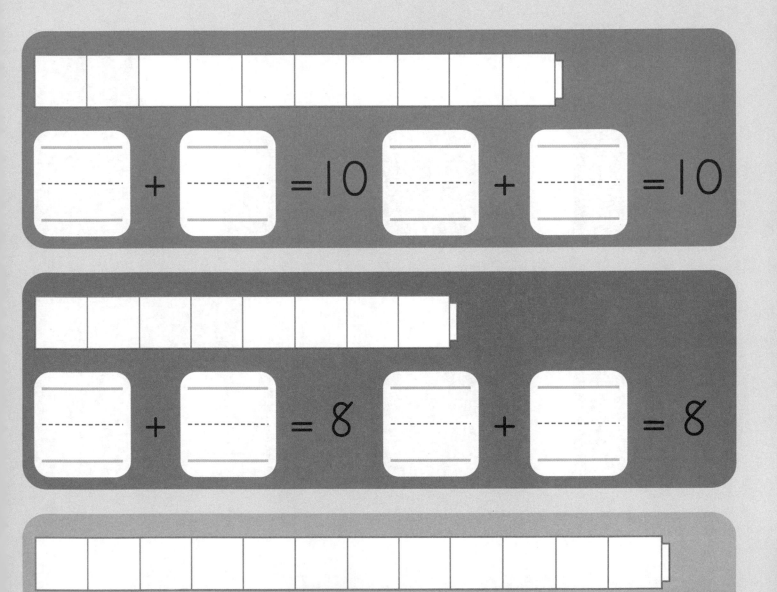

_____ + _____ = 10   _____ + _____ = 10

_____ + _____ = 8   _____ + _____ = 8

_____ + _____ = 12   _____ + _____ = 12

© Carson-Dellosa
CD-704462

Two-Color Sums

Use two different colors of counters to make each row. Then, write two addition facts that show the color amounts.

_____ + _____ = 11   _____ + _____ = 11

_____ + _____ = 9   _____ + _____ = 9

_____ + _____ = 13   _____ + _____ = 13

Dip into Dominoes

Count the dots on each side of each domino. Then, write the related facts for each domino.

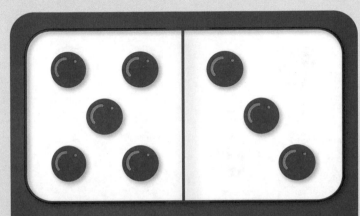

+ ___ = ___

+ ___ = ___

− ___ = ___

− ___ = ___

Dip into Dominoes

Count the dots on each side of each domino. Then, write the related facts for each domino.

+ _____ = _____

+ _____ = _____

− _____ = _____

− _____ = _____

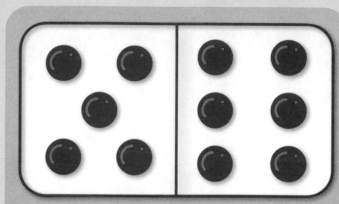

+ _____ = _____

+ _____ = _____

− _____ = _____

− _____ = _____

Subtraction Squares

Subtract each row and then each column. Write the answers on the lines.

11	6	_____
3	2	_____
_____	_____	_____

14	7	_____
5	4	_____
_____	_____	_____

16	8	_____
9	4	_____
_____	_____	_____

Subtraction Squares

Subtract each row and then each column. Write the answers on the lines.

10	4	____
3	2	____
____	____	____

13	8	____
5	4	____
____	____	____

15	7	____
9	4	____
____	____	____

Draw or cross out jelly beans in each frame to make the number.

Make 9

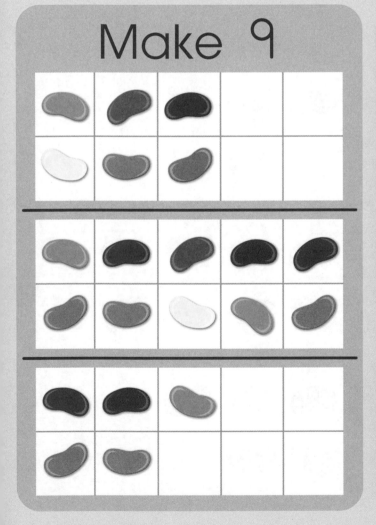

Make 6

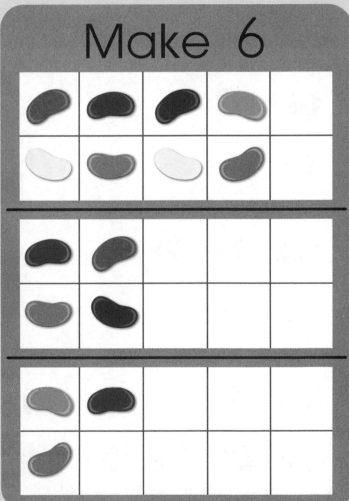

Jelly Bean Math

Draw or cross out jelly beans in each frame to make the number.

Make 7

Make 8

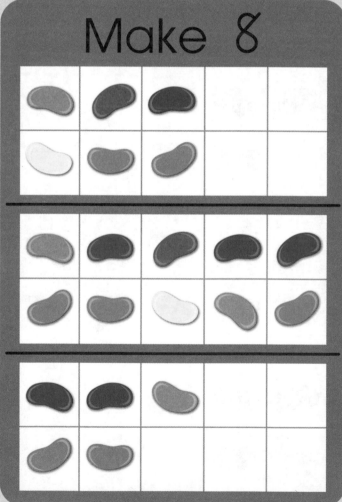

Thinking Kids™ Math
Grade 1

© Carson-Dellosa
CD-704462

Guess and Check

How many counters can you hold? Draw and write your estimate. Then, try it. Use the ten frames to count the counters. Write the actual number.

Estimate:

Actual:

A Number of Ways

Draw a picture of how you would model each number using base ten blocks. Write the number of tens and ones in the blanks.

tens	ones

tens	ones

_____ tens   _____ ones

_____ tens   _____ ones

A Number of Ways

Draw a picture of how you would model each number using base ten blocks. Write the number of tens and ones in the blanks.

tens	ones

tens	ones

_____ tens _____ ones

_____ tens _____ ones

© Carson-Dellosa
CD-704462

A Number of Ways

Draw a picture of how you would model each number using base ten blocks. Write the number of tens and ones in the blanks.

tens	ones

tens	ones

____ tens ____ ones   ____ tens ____ ones

Something Fishy

Choose two characteristics. Write them on the lines. Sort the fish by writing their numbers in the bowls.

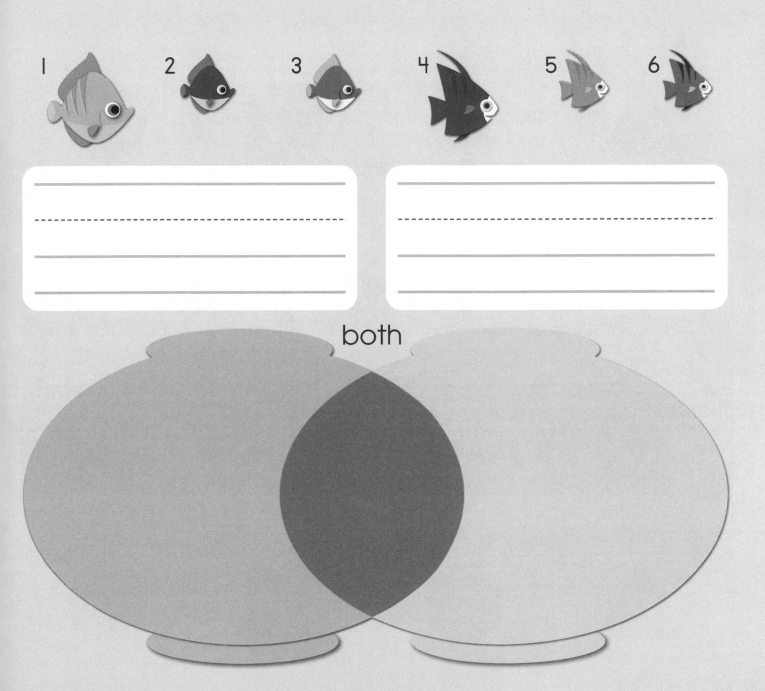

both

Thinking Kids™ Math
Grade 1

© Carson-Dellosa
CD-704462

Odd One Out

Draw an X on the object in each row that does not belong.

Quilt Patterns

Put counters on the squares in each row to make a pattern that matches.

Patterns, Patterns

Circle the object that comes next in each pattern.

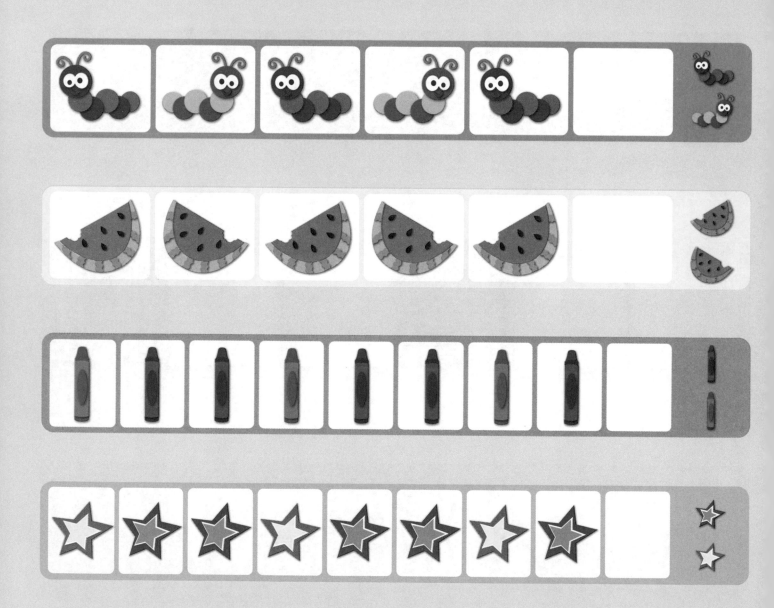

Put counters on the stems to complete each pattern.

Copy Cat

Name each pattern with the letters A and B. Then, use counters to copy the pattern.

Bead Patterns

Say each bead pattern. Then, answer the questions.

What color is the missing bead?

If this pattern continues, what color will the
15th bead be?

What color are the missing beads?

If this pattern continues, what color will the
12th bead be?

Keisha's Bracelets

Keisha made two bracelets. Use counters to show each pattern.

She made an AB pattern with 4  and 4 .

She made an ABC pattern with 3  , 3 , and 3 .

Each child named the shape pattern in a different way. Explain each child's rule.

Sara
A A B A A B A A B

Explain Sara's rule: _____

Gabe
A B C A B C A B C

Explain Gabe's rule: _____

Growing Patterns

Finish each pattern.

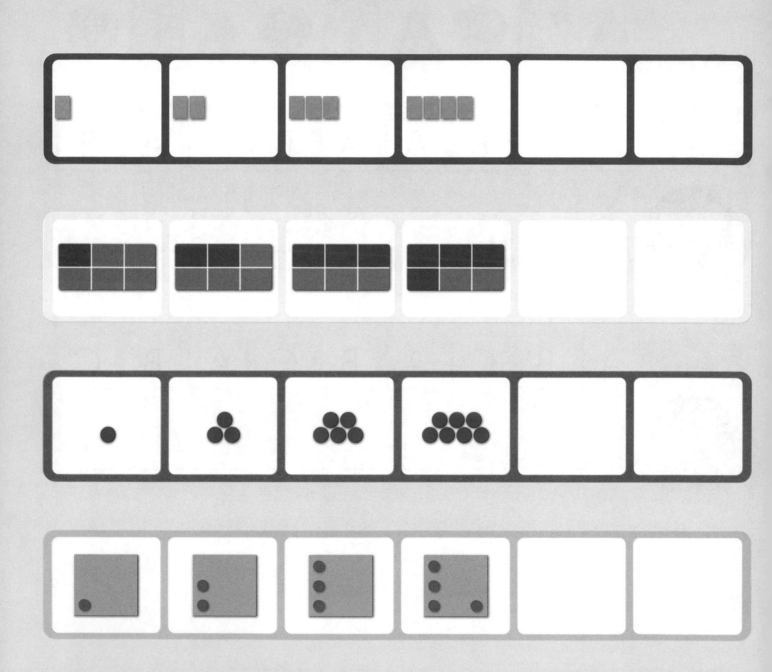

Draw what comes next in each pattern.

Puppy Patterns

Name each pattern using letters. Then, use counters to copy the pattern.

Draw the shape that comes next in each pattern. Tell whether the shape was slid, turned, or flipped.

Bead a Pattern

Put counters on the blank beads to continue each pattern.

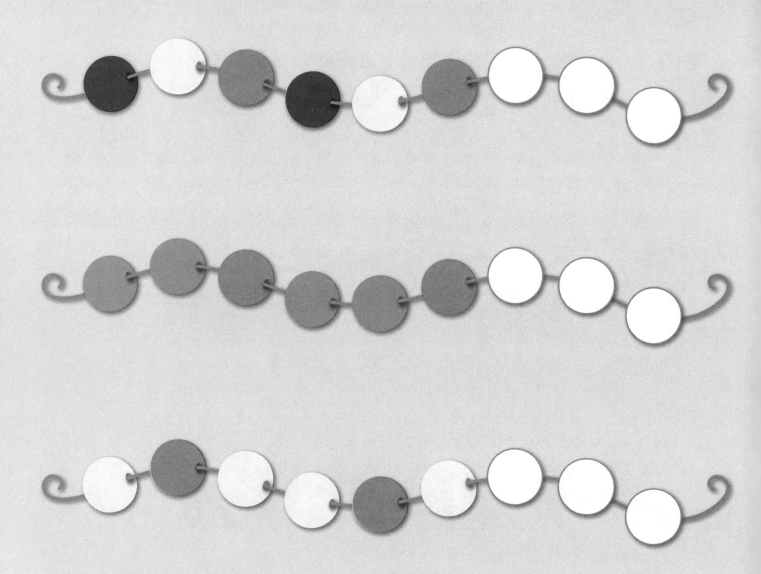

Finish each pattern.

© Carson-Dellosa
CD-704462

Finish each pattern.

Petal Patterns

Study each number pattern. Start at the dot. Write the rule.

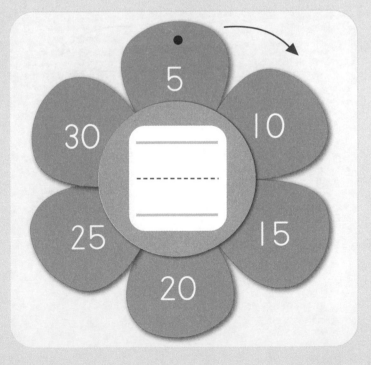

Petal Patterns

Study each number pattern. Start at the dot. Write the rule.

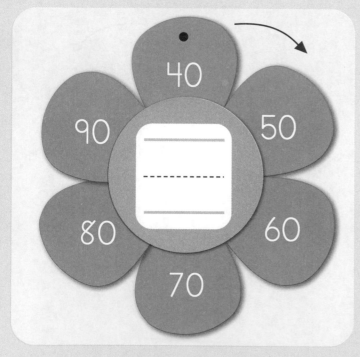

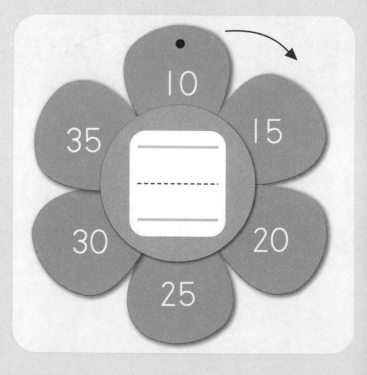

Buzzing Around

Write the missing numbers in each row of flowers.

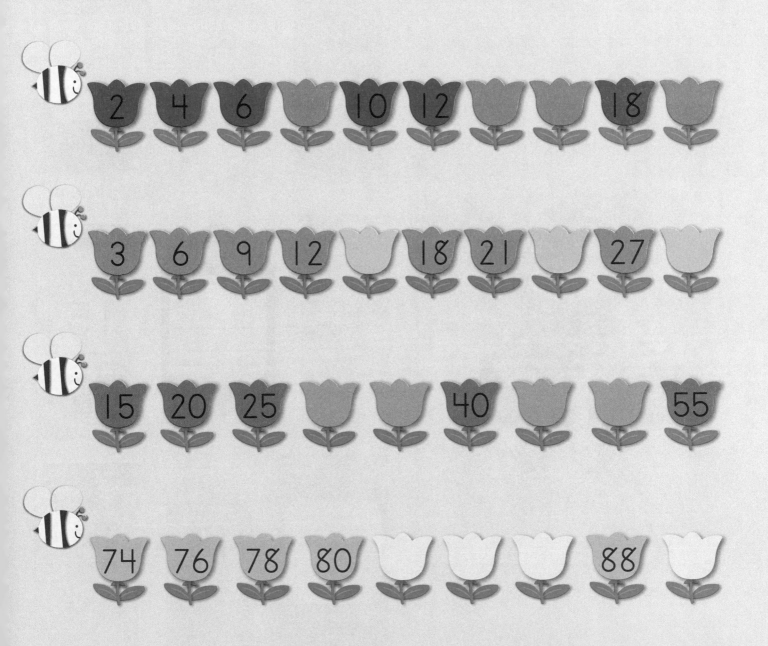

Row 1: 2, 4, 6, ___, 10, 12, ___, ___, 18, ___

Row 2: 3, 6, 9, 12, ___, 18, 21, ___, 27, ___

Row 3: 15, 20, 25, ___, ___, 40, ___, ___, 55

Row 4: 74, 76, 78, 80, ___, ___, ___, 88, ___

Thinking Kids™ Math
Grade 1

Zero the Hero

Write each missing number to complete the addition facts with zero.

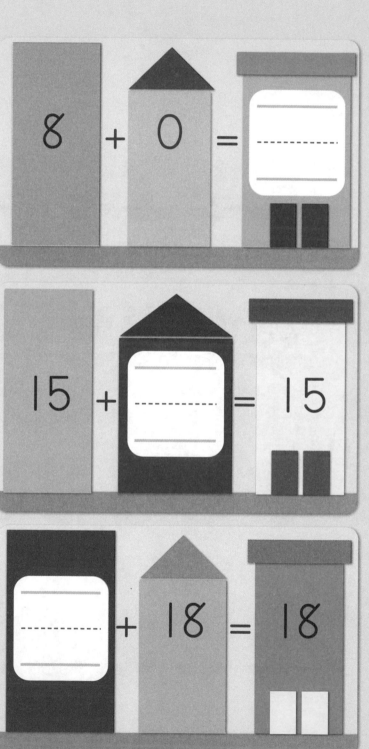

$8 + 0 = $ _____

$15 + $ _____ $ = 15$

_____ $ + 18 = 18$

Write each missing number to complete the addition facts with zero.

$11 + 0 =$ _____

_____ $+ 0 = 16$

$0 + 20 =$ _____

Switching and Staying

Put one domino on the left-hand side of each box. Count the dots and write the numbers on the lines. Then, turn the domino and repeat.

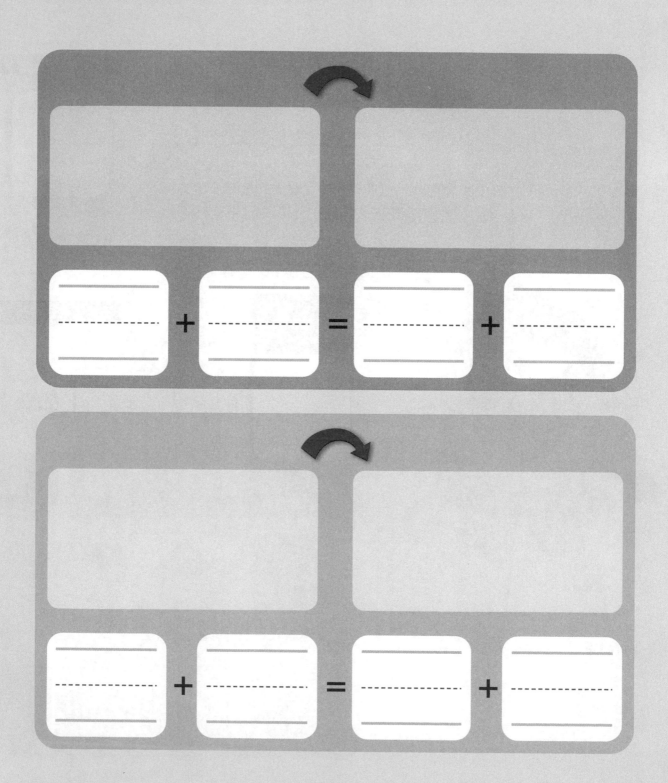

_____ + _____ = _____ + _____

_____ + _____ = _____ + _____

Bubble, Bubble

Put the same color of counters on each pair of bubbles that have the same sum.

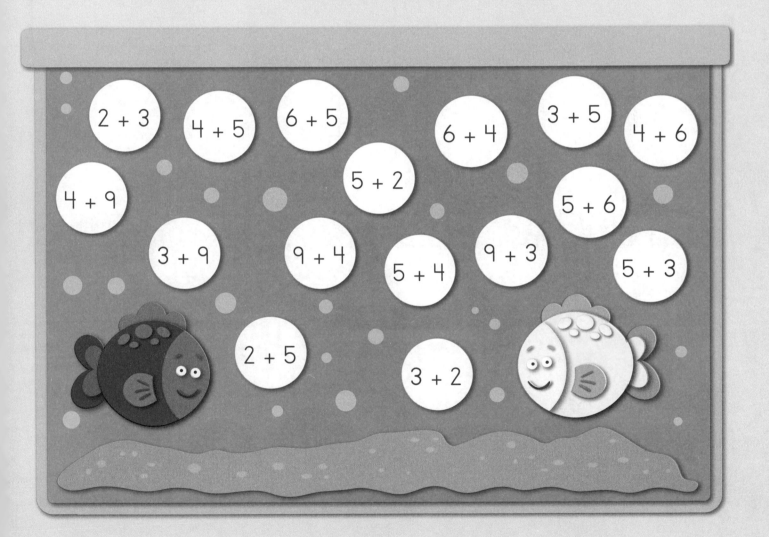

Put counters on each side of the seesaw to test each equation. Circle the equations that are true. Cross out the equations that are not true.

$5 + 4 = 6 + 3$ $5 + 1 = 4 + 3$ $4 + 4 = 5 + 3$

$4 + 6 = 2 + 8$ $3 + 7 = 8 + 2$ $2 + 3 = 6 + 0$

$1 + 5 = 3 + 3$ $6 + 1 = 3 + 4$ $2 + 6 = 5 + 2$

Tipping the Scales

Look at the numbers below each scale. Write >, <, or = to compare each set of numbers.

> greater than   **<** less than   **=** equal to

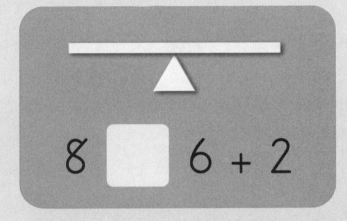

8 ☐ 6 + 2

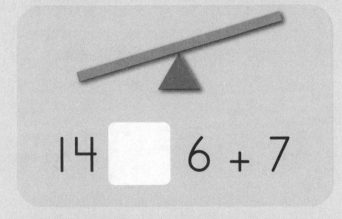

14 ☐ 6 + 7

12 ☐ 8 + 5

© Carson-Dellosa
CD-704462

Tipping the Scales

Look at the numbers below each scale. Write >, <, or = to compare each set of numbers.

> greater than   **<** less than   **=** equal to

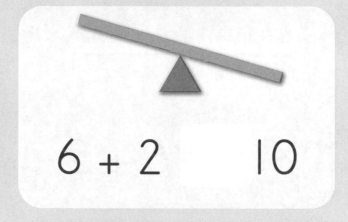

6 + 2   10

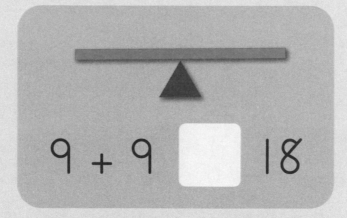

9 + 9 [ ] 18

13 [ ] 9 + 2

Circle the word that describes each object.

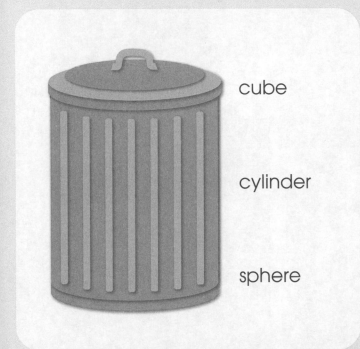

cube

cylinder

sphere

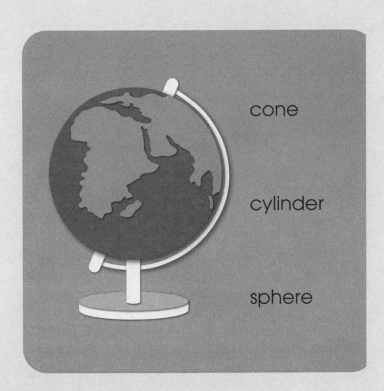

cone

cylinder

sphere

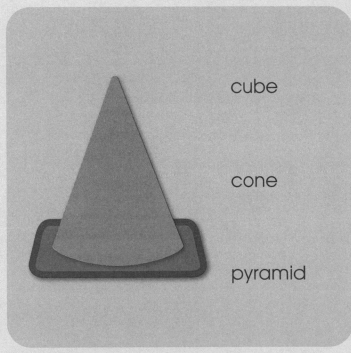

cube

cone

pyramid

Name That Figure!

Circle the word that describes each object.

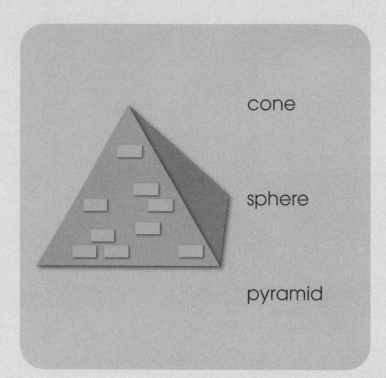

cone

sphere

pyramid

sphere

cone

rectangular prism

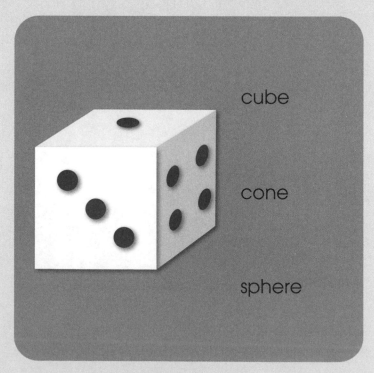

cube

cone

sphere

Shapes Rule!

Sort some counters by each rule. Then, write your own sorting rules and sort the blocks.

Straight Sides	Four Corners	
Curvy Sides	More or Less Than Four Corners	

The Great Shape Sort

Follow the directions.

1. Color each circle.

2. Outline each shape that has 4 sides.

3. Circle each small shape.

4. Draw an X on each square.

5. Draw a dot in each shape with 3 sides.

Thinking Kids™ Math
Grade 1

© Carson-Dellosa
CD-704462

Angles, Faces, and Sides

Read each description. Circle the correct figure. You may circle more than one figure in each row.

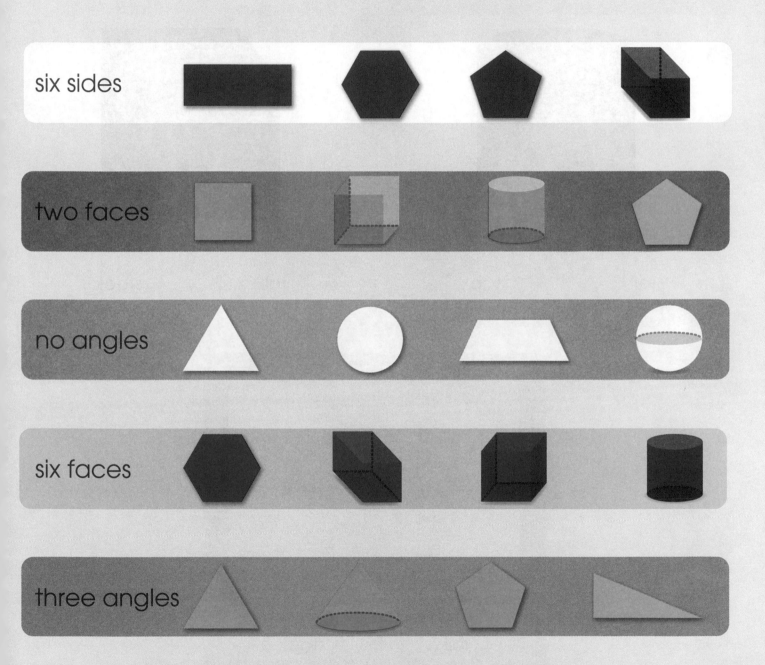

six sides

two faces

no angles

six faces

three angles

Stack and Roll

Look at each figure. Decide if it will roll, stack, or do both. Circle the answer(s).

roll   stack

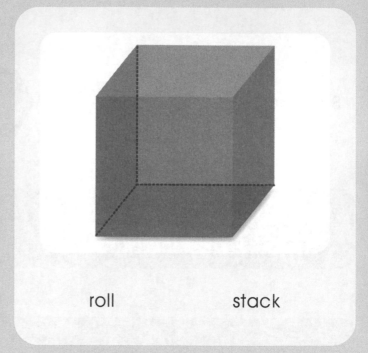

roll   stack

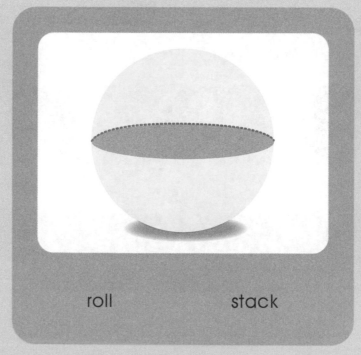

roll   stack

Stack and Roll

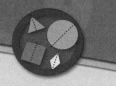

Look at each figure. Decide if it will roll, stack, or do both. Circle the answer(s).

roll   stack

roll   stack

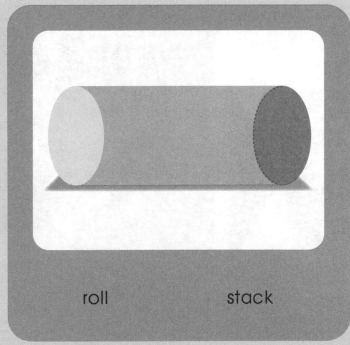

roll   stack

Shape Creations

Circle the shapes needed to make each picture.

Circle the shapes needed to make each picture.

Castle Shapes

Describe where each shape is using color words, shape names, and position words.

Beth's Beagle

Follow the directions to help Beth find her dog. Write the missing words in the directions as you go. Draw an X where she finds the dog.

Walk past 2 trees. Turn right and walk to the house.

Turn left and walk to the _____.

Turn right and walk to the _____.

Turn right and walk past the pond.

Turn right and walk to the _____.

Turn left and walk to the end of the garden.

Turn left and walk straight to find the dog.

The dog is in the _____.

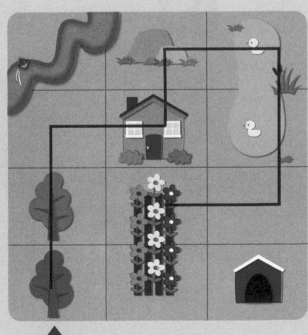

START

Where's the Bear?

Use numbers, letters, and shape names to describe where the bear is.

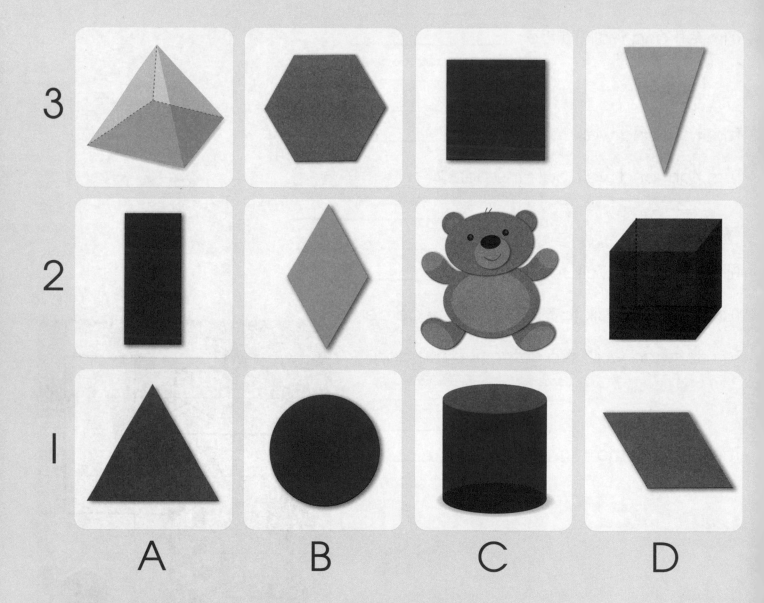

Flip, Slide, and Turn!

Place each block on its picture. Then, trace its flip, slide, and turn.

Shape	Flip	Slide	Turn
◀			

Circle the shapes and letters that have symmetry.

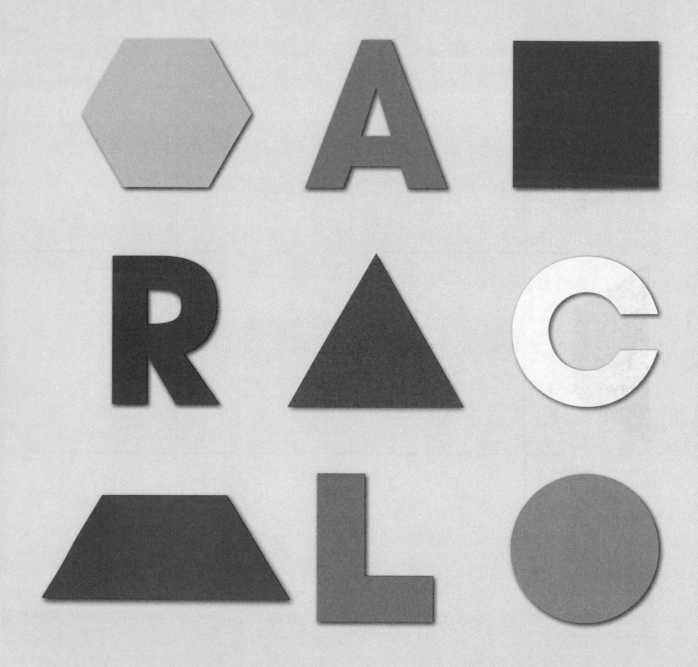

Circle each letter of the alphabet that has symmetry. Draw Xs on the letters that do not have symmetry.

A B C D E F

G H I J K L

M N O P Q R

S T U V W X

Y Z

Draw how each letter would look after a slide, a flip, and a turn.

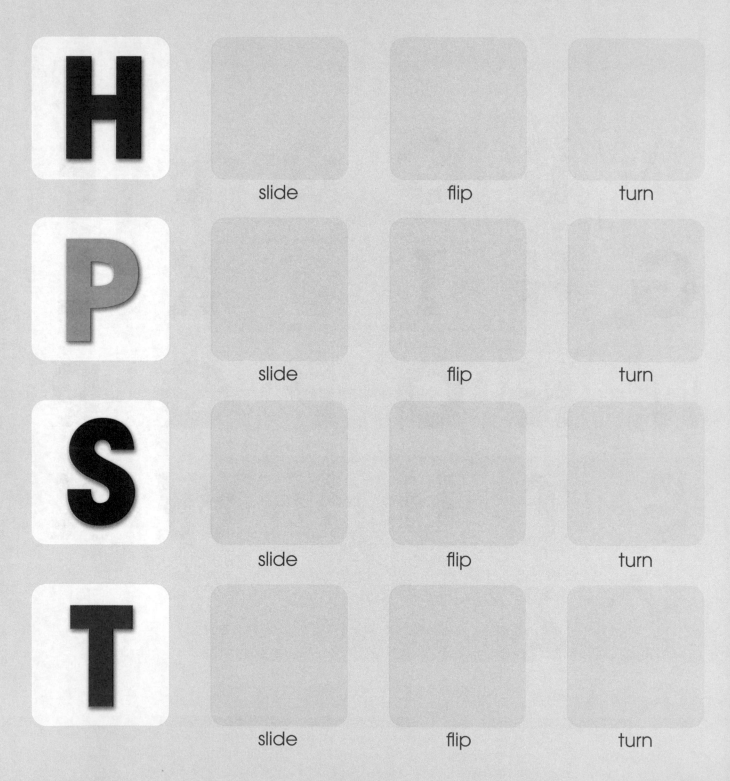

	slide	flip	turn
H			
P			
S			
T			

Circle the shape of the bottom face of each figure.

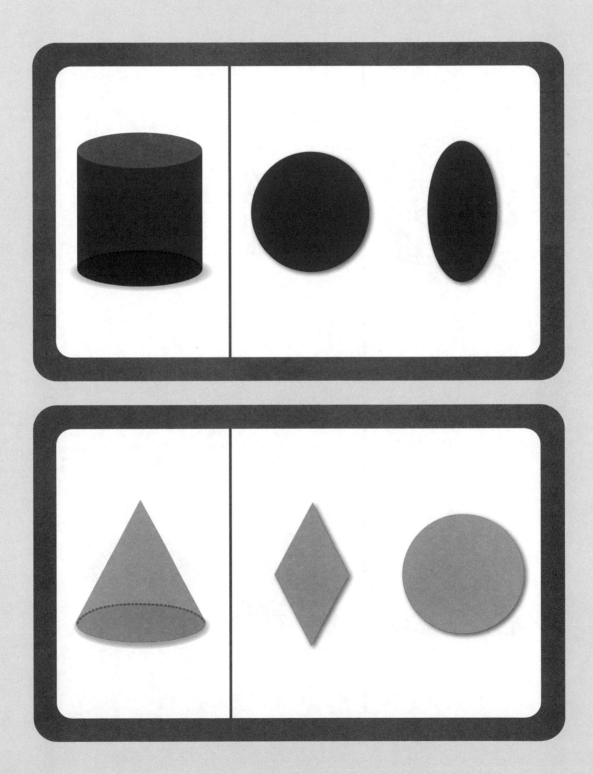

Find That Face!

Circle the shape of the bottom face of each figure.

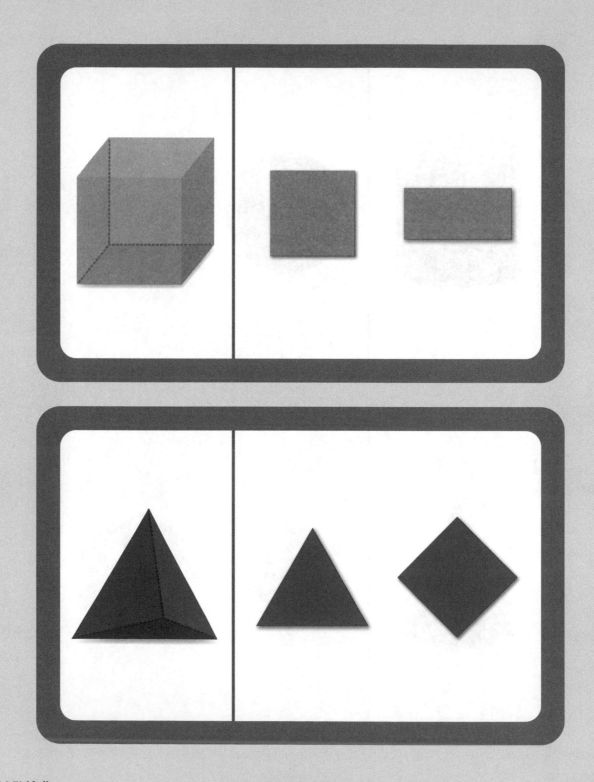

Picnic Perimeters

Write how many total steps it will take for each ant to walk around his picnic blanket.

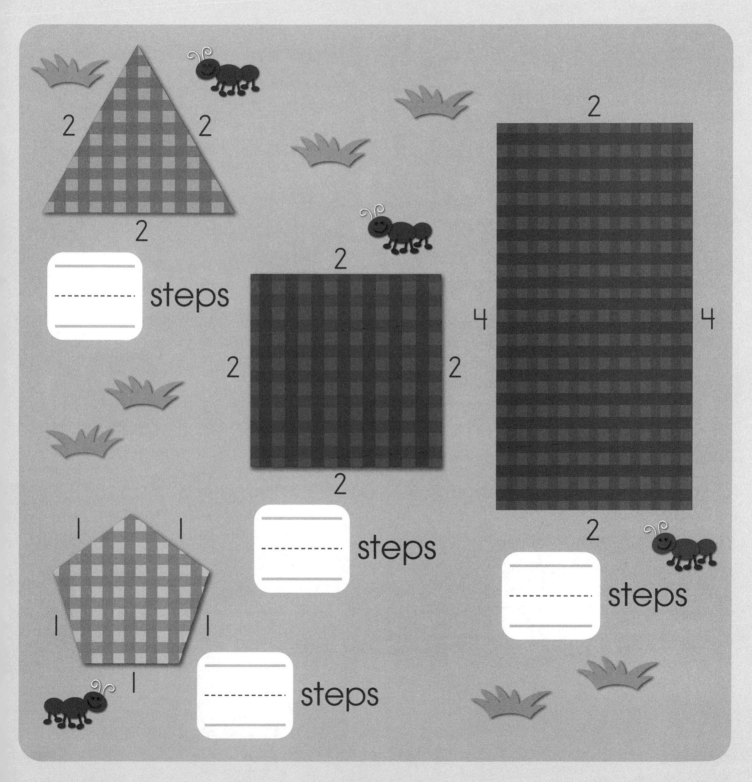

2   2

2

_____ steps

2

2   2

2

_____ steps

2

4   4

2

_____ steps

1   1

1   1

1

_____ steps

Measure It!

How long is your desk? Measure it with each object. Write the numbers.

markers

pencils

paper clips

cubes

counters

sheets of paper

Will found some worms in his backyard. Use two fingers at a time to measure each worm.

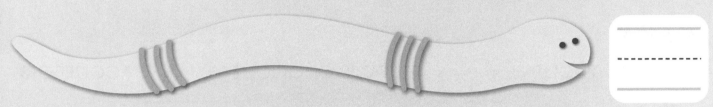

two-finger widths

two-finger widths

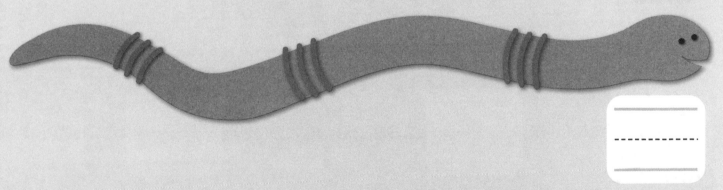

two-finger widths

two-finger widths

Pencils or Cubes?

Use unsharpened pencils to measure the length of each object. Then, use counters to measure the length of each object.

desk   about _____ pencils or about _____ counters

your arm   about _____ pencils or about _____ counters

book   about _____ pencils or about _____ counters

your shoe   about _____ pencils or about _____ counters

chair seat   about _____ pencils or about _____ counters

Measure the animals in inches and centimeters. Write each measurement on the line.

inches

centimeters

Animal Measures

Measure the animals in inches and centimeters. Write each measurement on the line.

inches

centimeters

Know Your Units

Circle the unit of measurement that best measures each object.

car

inch   foot

notebook

inch   foot

dog

inch   foot

shoe

centimeter   meter

paper clip

centimeter   meter

bee

centimeter   meter

Biggest Blankets

Use counters to find the area (A) of each blanket.

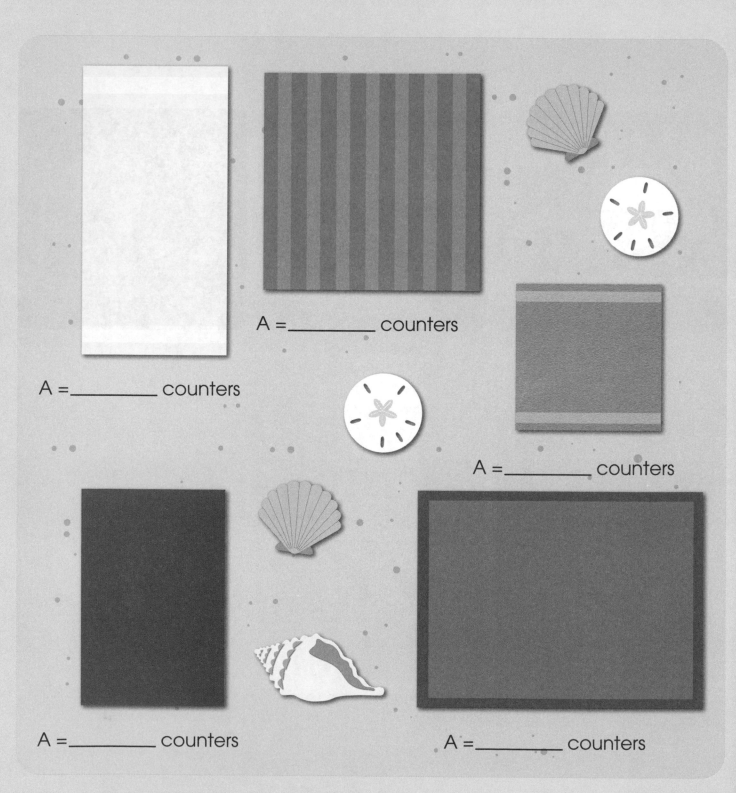

A =_____ counters

A =_____ counters

A =_____ counters

A =_____ counters

A =_____ counters

Measure Up!

Estimate the length of your desk. Then, measure your desk with each item.

Estimate: _____ paper clips long

Actual: _____ paper clips long

Estimate: _____ pencils long

Actual: _____ pencils long

Estimate: _____ paintbrushes long

Actual: _____ paintbrushes long

Estimate: _____ scissors long

Actual: _____ scissors long

Ribbon Measurement

Use the width of your thumb to measure the length of each ribbon.

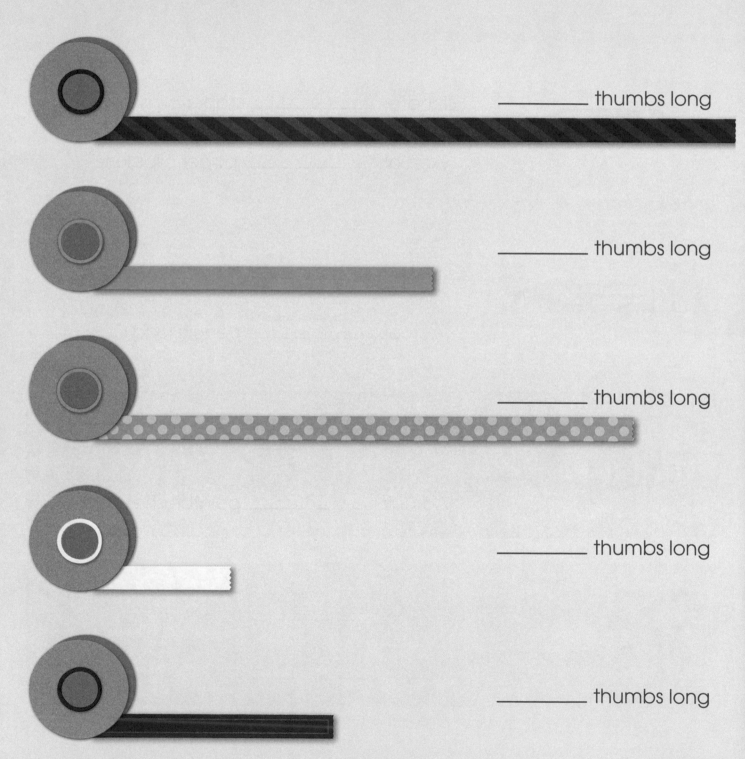

_____ thumbs long

_____ thumbs long

_____ thumbs long

_____ thumbs long

_____ thumbs long

Measure the length of each object with counters. Write the measurement on the line.

_____ counter(s)

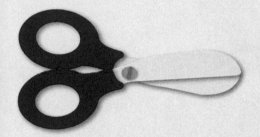

_____ counter(s)

_____ counter(s)

Buggy About Measurement

Measure the length of each bug with paper clips. Write the measurement on the line.

The ladybug is about _____ paper clips long.

The bee is about _____ paper clip long.

Order Up!

Number the events from 1 to 6 in the order in which they occur.

Eat breakfast.

Eat lunch.

Go to bed.

Go to school.

Wake up.

Eat dinner.

The Hands of Time

Draw the hands or write the numbers to show the time for each clock.

12:00

 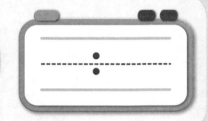

7:00

 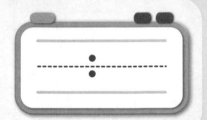

3:30

 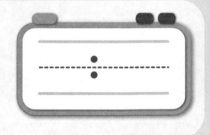

10:30

 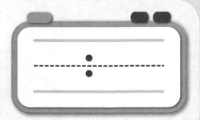

The Hands of Time

Draw the hands or write the numbers to show the time for each clock.

2:00

 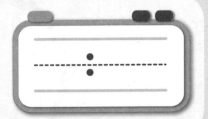

5:00

 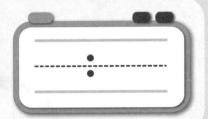

2:30

 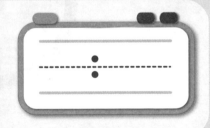

11:30

 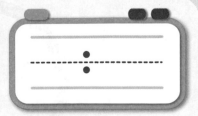

Time and Time Again

Read the times. Draw the hands and write the numbers for each time given.

five o'clock

one thirty

seven o'clock

Read the times. Draw the hands and write the numbers for each time given.

three thirty

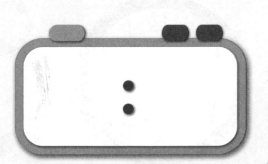

eight thirty

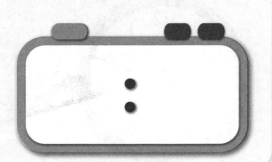

two o'clock

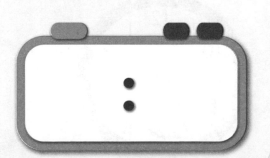

Time and Time Again

Read the times. Draw the hands and write the numbers for each time given.

six o'clock

two thirty

nine o'clock

Thinking Kids™ Math
Grade 1

Read the times. Draw the hands and write the numbers for each time given.

four thirty

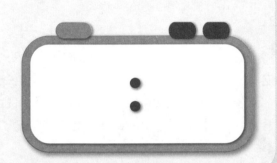

twelve thirty

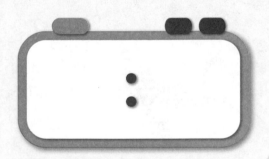

one o'clock

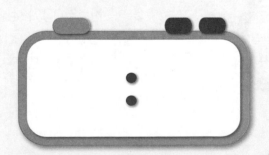

Elapsed Laps

Read each word problem. Draw the hands on the first clock to show the start time for the swimmer's laps. Draw the hands on the last clock to show the end time for the laps.

Start **End**

Katie arrived at swim practice at 3:30. She swam her warm-up laps in 30 minutes. What time did she finish?

Start **End**

Brady arrived at swim practice at 4:00. He finished his warm-up laps in 30 minutes. What time did he finish?

Start **End**

Ethan arrived at swim practice at 3:00. He finished his warm-up laps in 30 minutes. What time did he finish?

Elapsed Laps

Read each word problem. Draw the hands on the first clock to show the start time for the swimmer's laps. Draw the hands on the last clock to show the end time for the laps.

Start   **End**

 Jen arrived at swim practice at 4:30. She swam her warm-up laps in 30 minutes. What time did she finish?

Start   **End**

 Scott arrived at swim practice at 5:00. He finished his warm-up laps in 30 minutes. What time did he finish?

Start   **End**

 Adam arrived at swim practice at 2:30. He finished his warm-up laps in 30 minutes. What time did he finish?

© Carson-Dellosa
CD-704462

Number the animals from 1 to 6 to order them from lightest to heaviest.

chicken

frog

elephant

ant

dog

cow

Write the names of two objects or draw two objects on each scale to make the picture true.

Sorting Styles

Use buttons or counters of four different colors: blue, red, yellow, and black. Sort them into groups on the shirts by color.

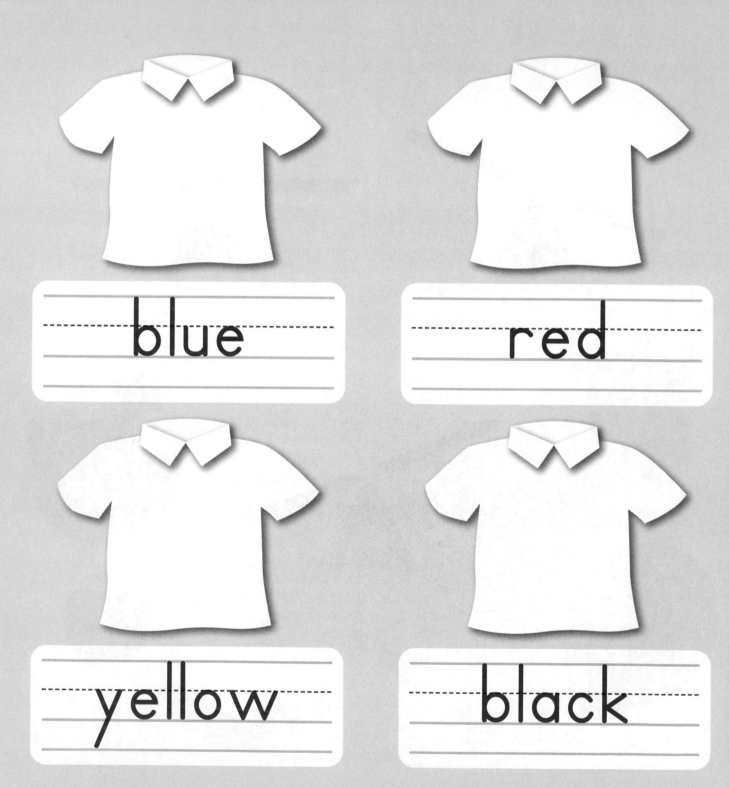

blue

red

yellow

black

Use buttons or counters of at least four different colors, sizes, and materials. Sort them into groups on the shirts. Write a word on the line to describe each group.

Shape Sorts

Put counters in each box that have something in common with the shape pictured.

Put counters in each box that have something in common with the shape pictured.

A Colorful Graph

Sort a handful of counters by color. Put them in the correct rows.

red					
blue					
yellow					
green					
orange					

Pencil Poll Pictograph

Jon took a poll of four friends to see how many pencils each had in his or her pencil box. Use Jon's tally chart to draw the pencils in the graph.

James	卌 I	Lisa	IIII
Tony	II	Anya	IIII

James						
James						
Tony						
Lisa						
Anya						

= I pencil

Balloon Poll Pictograph

Jane took a poll of four friends to see how many balloons each had. Use Jane's tally chart to draw the balloons in the graph.

Tom	|||	Jack	||||
Emily	ﷻﬀ		Maria	ﷻﬀ

Tom

Emily

Jack

Maria

🎈 = 1 balloon

Backyard Bugs

Lin counted the bugs she collected in her backyard. Draw Xs in the spaces above each bug to make a bar graph of her data.

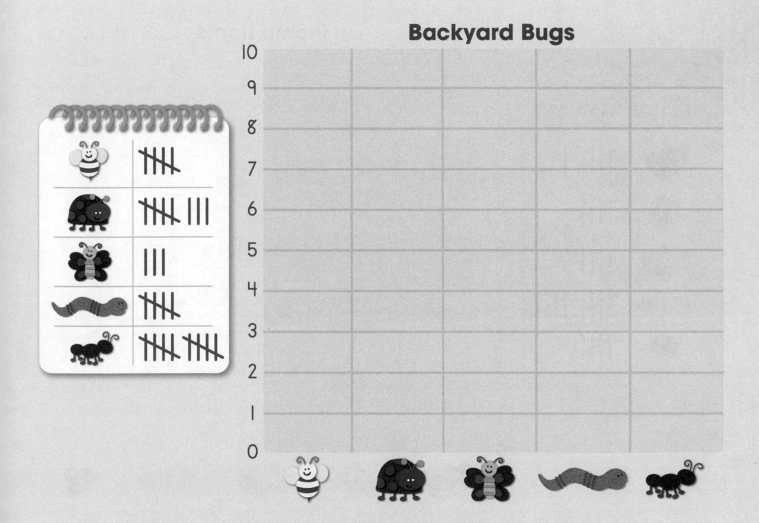

Picnic Time

Brian counted the items at the picnic. Draw Xs in the spaces above each item to make a bar graph of his data.

Preferred Pets

Look at the results of a class survey about favorite pets. Draw smiley faces to show the data in a pictograph. Look at the key to see how many votes each smiley face stands for.

‖‖ | ‖‖ ‖‖   ‖‖

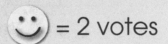 = 2 votes

Study the graph. Answer the questions.

What do the
pictures show?
    a. trees
    b. animals
    c. people

Write a title above
the graph.

Write two facts from the graph.

Sunny, Cloudy, or Rainy?

Mr. Kent's class kept track of the daily weather on the calendar last month. Use the calendar to answer the questions.

April

Sunday	Monday	Tuesday	Wednesday	Thursday	Friday	Saturday
					1	2
3	4	5	6	7	8	9
10	11	12	13	14	15	16
17	18	19	20	21	22	23
24	25	26	27	28	29	30

How many days were rainy? _____

How many days were cloudy but not rainy? _____

How many days were sunny? _____

How many days are in the month? _____

Likely or Unlikely?

Circle likely or unlikely to answer each question.

If you were playing a game with this spinner, is it **likely** or **unlikely** that you would spin red?

likely   unlikely

If you picked a marble out of this bag without looking, is it **likely** or **unlikely** that you would pick a red one?

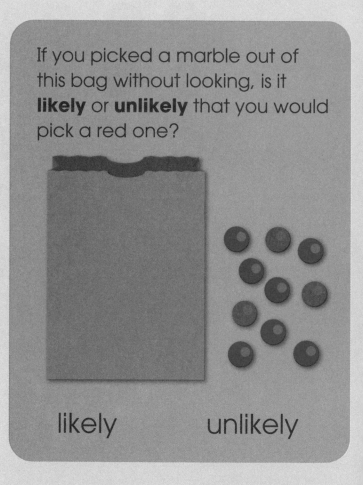

likely   unlikely

Wishing Well

Decide how likely it is that a tossed coin will land on each well. Below each well, write more likely, likely, or less likely.

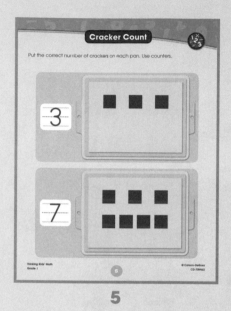

5

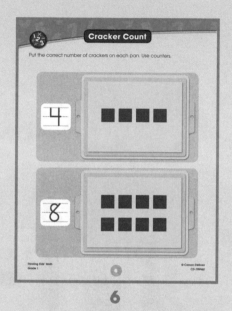

6

7

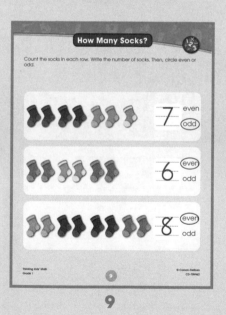

Catching Fish

Write a number. Catch that number of fish by circling the fish in the pond.

Answers will vary.

8

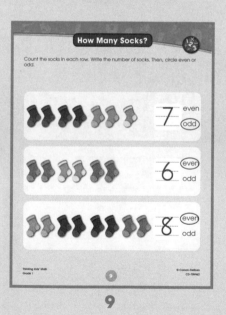

9

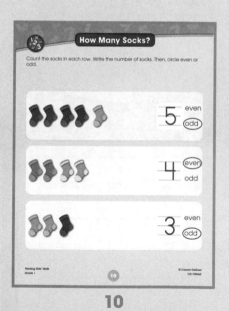

10

Answer Key

Clip Count

Make a chain with 23 paper clips. Separate the chains into groups of 10. Put each chain of 10 paper clips under tens. Put the leftovers under ones. Write the number of tens and ones and the total number of paper clips.

tens	ones
2 chains of 10 paper clips	3 paper clips

2 ten(s) and **3** one(s) is **23**

11

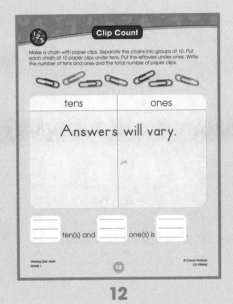

Clip Count

Make a chain with paper clips. Separate the chains into groups of 10. Put each chain of 10 paper clips under tens. Put the leftovers under ones. Write the number of tens and ones and the total number of paper clips.

tens	ones
Answers will vary.	

_____ ten(s) and _____ one(s) is _____

12

Balloon Bunches

Put a counter on each balloon. Write the number of tens and ones and the total. Draw balloons to show and write the total in the last box.

1 ten
6 ones
16 total

1 ten
9 ones
19 total

2 tens
4 ones
24 total

13

Balloon Bunches

Put a counter on each balloon. Write the number of tens and ones and the total. Draw balloons to show and write the total in the last box.

1 ten
4 ones
14 total

1 ten
7 ones
17 total

2 tens
3 ones
23 total

14

Balloon Bunches

Put a counter on each balloon. Write the number of tens and ones and the total. Draw balloons to show and write the total in the last box.

1 ten
8 ones
18 total

1 ten
5 ones
15 total

2 tens
2 ones
22 total

15

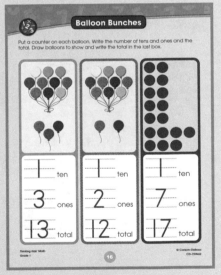

Balloon Bunches

Put a counter on each balloon. Write the number of tens and ones and the total. Draw balloons to show and write the total in the last box.

1 ten
3 ones
13 total

1 ten
2 ones
12 total

1 ten
7 ones
17 total

16

17

Pinball Numbers

Write numbers to complete the chart. Use counters to help you. The first one has been done for you.

23
2 tens 3 ones
20 + 3
23

46
4 tens 6 ones
40 + 6
46

18

Pinball Numbers

Write numbers to complete the charts. Use counters to help you.

32
3 tens 2 ones
30 + 2
32

78
7 tens 8 ones
70 + 8
78

19

Pinball Numbers

Write numbers to complete the charts. Use counters to help you.

82
8 tens 2 ones
80 + 2
82

96
9 tens 6 ones
90 + 6
96

20

Pinball Numbers

Write numbers to complete the charts. Use counters to help you.

57
5 tens 7 ones
50 + 7
57

63
6 tens 3 ones
60 + 3
63

21

Peas and Carrots

Count the peas and carrots. Circle groups of 10. Write how many tens and ones. Write the total. Then, answer the question.

__6__ tens and __2__ ones is __62__ peas and carrots.

How can you write the total in other ways?

__5__ tens and __12__ ones

__4__ tens and __22__ ones

22

Traffic Jam

Put cars on the street. Use counters. Write the missing number under each car.

- A red car is 1st.
- A blue car is 4th.
- A green car is 10th.
- A brown car is 3rd.
- A black car is 7th.
- A white car is 9th.

1 2 3 4 5 6 7 8 9 10

Answer Key

Traffic Jam

Put cars on the street. Use counters. Write the missing number under each car.

- An orange car is 2nd.
- A pink car is 5th.
- A purple car is 8th.
- A gray car is 6th.

1 2 3 4 5 6 7 8 9 10

23

Speedy Snails

Write the number on the shell or the ordinal number word on the line to show the order the snails will finish the race.

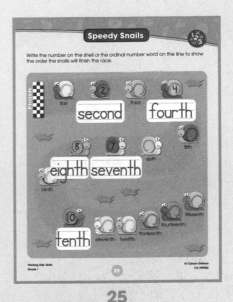

first — 1
second — 2
third
fourth — 4
fifth — 5
sixth — 6
seventh
eighth
ninth — 9
tenth — 10
eleventh
twelfth
thirteenth
fourteenth
fifteenth

24

Speedy Snails

Write the number on the shell or the ordinal number word on the line to show the order the snails will finish the race.

first
second — 2
third
fourth — 4
fifth
sixth
seventh — 7
eighth — 8
ninth
tenth — 10
eleventh
twelfth
thirteenth
fourteenth
fifteenth

25

Puppy Playtime

Help the puppy count to 100. Write the number that is hidden under each object.

17
25
61
74
80

26

Puppy Playtime

Help the puppy count to 100. Write the number that is hidden under each object.

13
27
44
68
82

27

Square Subtraction

Use the hundred board to solve each problem. Circle the first number in the problem on the board. Then, draw a path on the board as you count back to subtract the second number. Draw a triangle around the answer. Write the answer to complete the number sentence.

$22 - 11 = 11$ $67 - 14 = 53$ $36 - 9 = 27$

$88 - 12 = 76$ $94 - 5 = 89$ $51 - 12 = 39$

28

Answer Key

Shake and Spill

Put 5 counters in a cup. Shake and spill them onto the page. Write 4 number sentences describing the counters.

Answers will vary.

___ + ___ = ___   ___ + ___ = ___

___ + ___ = ___   ___ + ___ = ___

29

Shake and Spill

Put 10 counters in a cup. Shake and spill them onto the page. Write 4 number sentences describing the counters.

Answers will vary.

___ + ___ = ___   ___ + ___ = ___

___ + ___ = ___   ___ + ___ = ___

30

Filling Flower Beds

Look at the number. Put counters in the 2 flower beds to show the number. Remove the counters and draw that number of flowers.

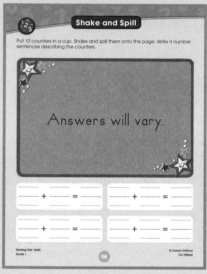

31

Filling Flower Beds

Look at the number. Put counters in the 2 flower beds to show the number. Remove the counters and draw that number of flowers.

32

The More Door

Draw a door around the number that is greater on each house.

33

The More Door

Draw a door around the number that is greater on each house.

34

Answer Key

The More Door
Draw a door around the number that is greater on each house.

43 **34** | **67** 76 | **91** 19
58 **85** | 79 **97**

35

The More Door
Draw a door around the number that is greater on each house.

29 **92** | 35 **53** | 46 **64**
86 68 | **51** 15

36

TV Sets
Read each number. Circle the correct number word. Show the number in 2 different ways using pictures, number sentences, or tally marks.

5 Answers will vary.
three   seven   (five)

9 Answers will vary.
(nine)   zero   three

14 Answers will vary.
sixteen   (fourteen)   four

16 Answers will vary.
eleven   (sixteen)   twelve

37

TV Sets
Read each number. Circle the correct number word. Show the number in 2 different ways using pictures, number sentences, or tally marks.

6 Answers will vary.
four   (six)   seven

11 Answers will vary.
nine   zero   (eleven)

15 Answers will vary.
five   (fifteen)   four

17 Answers will vary.
eleven   sixteen   (seventeen)

38

Bubble Count
Count the bubbles in each bathtub. Write the number on the line. Circle the correct number word.

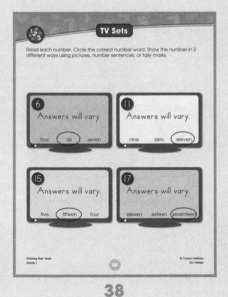

16 (sixteen) sixty
20 twelve (twenty)
15 fifty (fifteen)
19 (nineteen) ninety

39

Bubble Count
Count the bubbles in each bathtub. Write the number on the line. Circle the correct number word.

17 (seventeen) seventy
13 (thirteen) thirty
14 forty (fourteen)
18 (eighteen) eighty

40

41

By the Slice

Circle each pizza that shows equal parts.

42

Fraction Snacks

Draw lines to divide each snack into equal parts to show the bottom number of the fraction. Draw an X on one part to show the fraction.

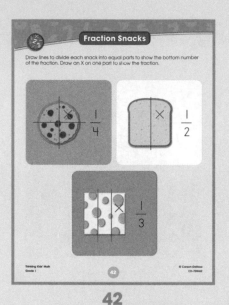

43

Fraction Snacks

Draw lines to divide each snack into equal parts to show the bottom number of the fraction. Draw an X on one part to show the fraction.

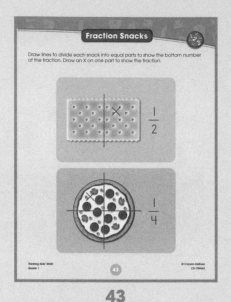

44

Apple Picking

Write the fractions of red and yellow apples in each tree. The first two have been started for you.

red	yellow	red	yellow	red	yellow
5	2	4	4	3	2
7	7	8	8	5	5

45

Apple Picking

Write the fractions of red and yellow apples in each tree.

red	yellow	red	yellow	red	yellow
7	2	4	6	6	5
9	9	10	10	11	11

46

Nest Sets

Look at the numbers below the first and second nests. Put eggs in the nests to show the numbers use counters. Move the eggs to the last nest. Write the sum.

$$4 + 3 = 7$$

Answer Key

Nest Sets

Write a number below the first and second nests. Put eggs in the nests to show the numbers use counters. Move the eggs to the last nest. Write the sum.

Answers will vary.

Thinking Kids' Math
Grade 1
47
© Carson-Dellosa
CD-704462

47

Planting On

Count the vegetables in each row. Put a counter in each box and count on to make the sum at the end of each row.

12

9

14

Thinking Kids' Math
Grade 1
48
© Carson-Dellosa
CD-704462

48

Planting On

Count the vegetables in each row. Put a counter in each box and count on to make the sum at the end of each row.

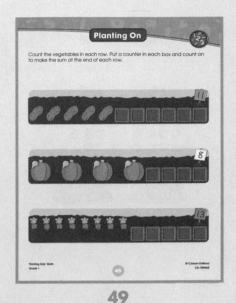

11

8

13

Thinking Kids' Math
Grade 1
49
© Carson-Dellosa
CD-704462

49

Bears' Lair

Put 8 bears in the cave. Use counters. Roll the die and subtract that many bears. Write the number sentence. Repeat three more times.

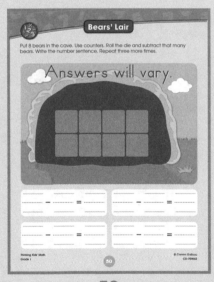

Answers will vary.

Thinking Kids' Math
Grade 1
50
© Carson-Dellosa
CD-704462

50

Bears' Lair

Put 10 bears in the cave. Use counters. Roll the die and subtract that many bears. Write the number sentence. Repeat three more times.

Answers will vary.

Thinking Kids' Math
Grade 1
51
© Carson-Dellosa
CD-704462

51

Frogs on a Log

Roll a die. Starting at 10, count back the rolled number as hops on the log. Write what you did as a subtraction fact. Repeat five more times.

Answers will vary.

1 2 3 4 5 6 7 8 9 10

Thinking Kids' Math
Grade 1
52
© Carson-Dellosa
CD-704462

52

Answer Key

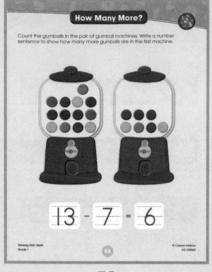

How Many More?

Count the gumballs in the pair of gumball machines. Write a number sentence to show how many more gumballs are in the first machine.

$$13 - 7 = 6$$

Thinking Kids' Math
Grade 1

© Carson-Dellosa
CD-704462

53

How Many More?

Count the gumballs in the pair of gumball machines. Write a number sentence to show how many more gumballs are in the first machine.

$$11 - 6 = 5$$

Thinking Kids' Math
Grade 1

© Carson-Dellosa
CD-704462

54

Blastoff Facts

Write the four facts for each fact family.

6, 9, 15

$$6 + 9 = 15$$
$$9 + 6 = 15$$
$$15 - 9 = 6$$
$$15 - 6 = 9$$

4, 8, 12

$$4 + 8 = 12$$
$$8 + 4 = 12$$
$$12 - 8 = 4$$
$$12 - 4 = 8$$

Thinking Kids' Math
Grade 1

© Carson-Dellosa
CD-704462

55

Blastoff Facts

Write the four facts for each fact family.

6, 7, 13

$$6 + 7 = 13$$
$$7 + 6 = 13$$
$$13 - 6 = 7$$
$$13 - 7 = 6$$

8, 9, 17

$$8 + 9 = 17$$
$$9 + 8 = 17$$
$$17 - 9 = 8$$
$$17 - 8 = 9$$

Thinking Kids' Math
Grade 1

© Carson-Dellosa
CD-704462

56

Seeing Spots

Look at the domino in each box. Each domino represents a fact family. Then, write the related facts for each fact family.

$$5 + 4 = 9$$
$$4 + 5 = 9$$
$$9 - 5 = 4$$
$$9 - 4 = 5$$

$$6 + 2 = 8$$
$$2 + 6 = 8$$
$$8 - 6 = 2$$
$$8 - 2 = 6$$

Thinking Kids' Math
Grade 1

© Carson-Dellosa
CD-704462

57

Seeing Spots

Look at the domino in each box. Each domino represents a fact family. Then, write the related facts for each fact family.

$$3 + 1 = 4$$
$$1 + 3 = 4$$
$$4 - 1 = 3$$
$$4 - 3 = 1$$

$$4 + 3 = 7$$
$$3 + 4 = 7$$
$$7 - 4 = 3$$
$$7 - 3 = 4$$

Thinking Kids' Math
Grade 1

© Carson-Dellosa
CD-704462

58

Answer Key

Baskets of Cherries

Three children picked cherries. Add the three amounts of cherries that each child picked.

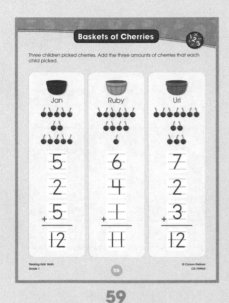

Jan
```
  5
  2
+ 5
 12
```

Ruby
```
  6
  4
+ 1
 11
```

Uri
```
  7
  2
+ 3
 12
```

59

Baskets of Cherries

Three children picked cherries. Add the three amounts of cherries that each child picked.

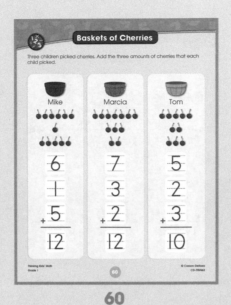

Mike
```
  6
  1
+ 5
 12
```

Marcia
```
  7
  3
+ 2
 12
```

Tom
```
  5
  2
+ 3
 10
```

60

Mystery Signs

Write + or – to make each number sentence true.

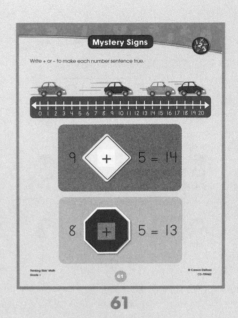

$9 + 5 = 14$

$8 + 5 = 13$

61

Mystery Signs

Write + or – to make each number sentence true.

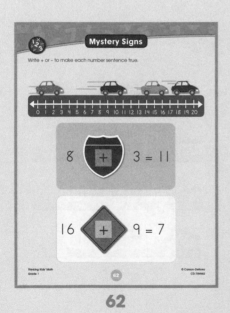

$8 + 3 = 11$

$16 - 9 = 7$

62

Let's Share!

Put a counter on each acorn and each peanut. Divide each set of nuts into two equal groups so that the squirrels will have equal shares.

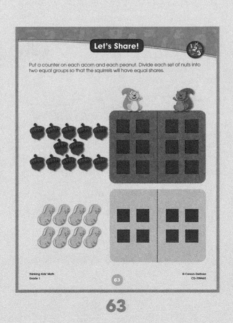

63

Let's Share!

Put a counter on each acorn and each peanut. Divide each set of nuts into two equal groups so that the squirrels will have equal shares.

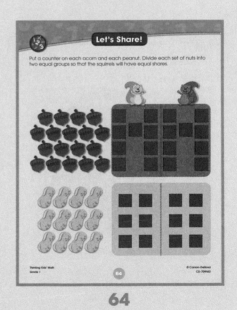

64

Answer Key

Seeing Double

Roll a die and draw the dots in the box. Then, use the number to write a doubles fact number sentence. The first one has been done for you.

$5 + 5 = 10$

Answers will vary.

65

Adventure Island

Count on to solve each problem. The common sum is the spot where the pirate buried his treasure. Mark the spot on the number line with an X.

10	14	16	11	9	15
+ 8	+ 4	+ 2	+ 7	+ 9	+ 3
18	18	18	18	18	18

66

Adventure Island

Count on to solve each problem. The common sum is the spot where the pirate buried his treasure. Mark the spot on the number line with an X.

10	12	14	11	8	13
+ 6	+ 4	+ 2	+ 5	+ 8	+ 3
16	16	16	16	16	16

67

Count Back to Takeoff!

Put 20 counters on the rocket. Count back from 20 by rolling one die and removing that number of counters.

Answers will vary.

68

Flip It!

Solve each addition problem. Use the addition facts to help you solve each subtraction problem.

$18 - 9 = 9$ THINK $9 + 9 = 18$

$14 - 6 = 8$ THINK $6 + 8 = 14$

$17 - 8 = 9$ THINK $8 + 9 = 17$

$15 - 7 = 8$ THINK $7 + 8 = 15$

69

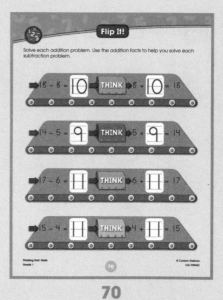

Flip It!

Solve each addition problem. Use the addition facts to help you solve each subtraction problem.

$18 - 8 = 10$ THINK $8 + 10 = 18$

$14 - 5 = 9$ THINK $5 + 9 = 14$

$17 - 6 = 11$ THINK $6 + 11 = 17$

$15 - 4 = 11$ THINK $4 + 11 = 15$

70

Thinking Kids™ Math
Grade 1

© Carson-Dellosa
CD-704462

Answer Key

More or Less

Start with the middle number. Write the numbers that are 1 more and 2 more. Then, write the numbers that are 1 less and 2 less.

-2	-1		+1	+2
5	6	7	8	9
8	9	10	11	12
13	14	15	16	17

Thinking Kids' Math
Grade 1
71
© Carson-Dellosa
CD-704462

71

More or Less

Start with the middle number. Write the numbers that are 1 more and 2 more. Then, write the numbers that are 1 less and 2 less.

-2	-1		+1	+2
6	7	8	9	10
9	10	11	12	13
11	12	13	14	15

Thinking Kids' Math
Grade 1
72
© Carson-Dellosa
CD-704462

72

Two-Color Sums

Use two different colors of counters to make each row. Then, write two addition facts that show the color amounts.

Answers will vary.

___ + ___ = 10   ___ + ___ = 10

___ + ___ = 8   ___ + ___ = 8

___ + ___ = 12   ___ + ___ = 12

Thinking Kids' Math
Grade 1
73
© Carson-Dellosa
CD-704462

73

Two-Color Sums

Use two different colors of counters to make each row. Then, write two addition facts that show the color amounts.

Answers will vary.

___ + ___ = 11   ___ + ___ = 11

___ + ___ = 9   ___ + ___ = 9

___ + ___ = 13   ___ + ___ = 13

Thinking Kids' Math
Grade 1
74
© Carson-Dellosa
CD-704462

74

Dip into Dominoes

Count the dots on each side of each domino. Then, write the related facts for each domino.

$2 + 4 = 6$ $5 + 3 = 8$
$4 + 2 = 6$ $3 + 5 = 8$
$6 - 2 = 4$ $8 - 3 = 5$
$6 - 4 = 2$ $8 - 5 = 3$

Thinking Kids' Math
Grade 1
75
© Carson-Dellosa
CD-704462

75

Dip into Dominoes

Count the dots on each side of each domino. Then, write the related facts for each domino.

$3 + 4 = 7$ $5 + 6 = 11$
$4 + 3 = 7$ $6 + 5 = 11$
$7 - 3 = 4$ $11 - 5 = 6$
$7 - 4 = 3$ $11 - 6 = 5$

Thinking Kids' Math
Grade 1
76
© Carson-Dellosa
CD-704462

76

Answer Key

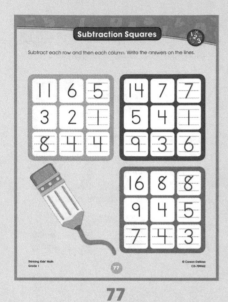

77

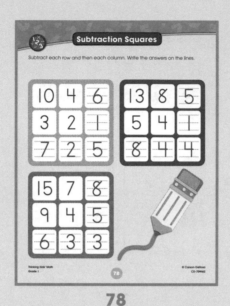

78

79

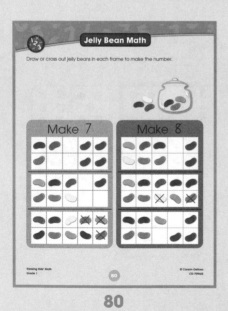

80

Guess and Check

How many counters can you hold? Draw and write your estimate. Then, try it. Use the ten frames to count the counters. Write the actual number.

Answers will vary.

Estimate: ___ Actual: ___

81

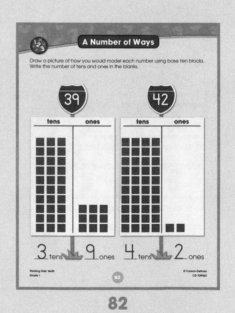

A Number of Ways

Draw a picture of how you would model each number using base ten blocks. Write the number of tens and ones in the blanks.

3 tens 9 ones   4 tens 2 ones

82

Answer Key

A Number of Ways

Draw a picture of how you would model each number using base ten blocks. Write the number of tens and ones in the blanks.

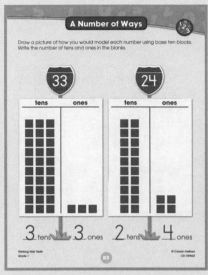

3 tens **3** ones **2** tens **4** ones

Thinking Kids' Math
Grade 1

83

© Carson-Dellosa
CD-704462

83

A Number of Ways

Draw a picture of how you would model each number using base ten blocks. Write the number of tens and ones in the blanks.

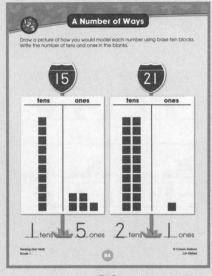

1 tens **5** ones **2** tens **1** ones

Thinking Kids' Math
Grade 1

84

© Carson-Dellosa
CD-704462

84

Something Fishy

Choose two characteristics. Write them on the lines. Sort the fish by writing their numbers in the bowls.

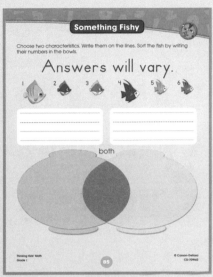

Answers will vary.

Thinking Kids' Math
Grade 1

85

© Carson-Dellosa
CD-704462

85

Odd One Out

Draw an X on the object in each row that does not belong.

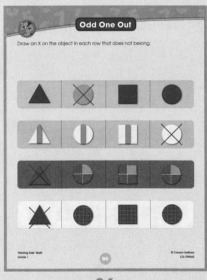

Thinking Kids' Math
Grade 1

86

© Carson-Dellosa
CD-704462

86

Quilt Patterns

Put counters on the squares in each row to make a pattern that matches.

Answers will vary.

Thinking Kids' Math
Grade 1

87

© Carson-Dellosa
CD-704462

87

Patterns, Patterns

Circle the object that comes next in each pattern.

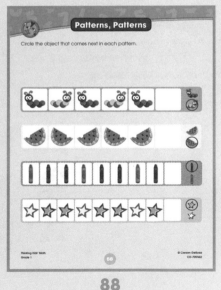

Thinking Kids' Math
Grade 1

88

© Carson-Dellosa
CD-704462

88

Thinking Kids™ Math
Grade 1

179

© Carson-Dellosa
CD-704462

A Garden of Patterns

Put counters on the stems to complete each pattern.

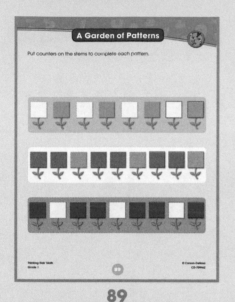

89

Copy Cat

Name each pattern with the letters A and B. Then, use counters to copy the pattern.

A B A B A B

A B B A B B

90

Bead Patterns

Say each bead pattern. Then, answer the questions.

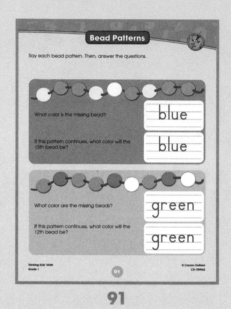

What color is the missing bead? **blue**

If this pattern continues, what color will the 15th bead be? **blue**

What color are the missing beads? **green**

If this pattern continues, what color will the 12th bead be? **green**

91

Keisha's Bracelets

Keisha made two bracelets. Use counters to show each pattern.

Answers will vary.

She made an AB pattern with 4 ● and 4 ●.

She made an ABC pattern with 3 ●, 3 ●, and 3 ○.

92

Patterns Rule!

Each child named the shape pattern in a different way. Explain each child's rule.

Sara   A A B A A B A A B

Explain Sara's rule: **blue blue red**

Gabe   A B C A B C A B C

Explain Gabe's rule: **triangle square circle**

93

Growing Patterns

Finish each pattern.

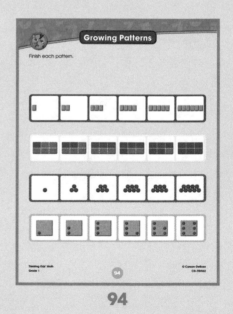

94

Answer Key

What's the Rule?

Draw what comes next in each pattern.

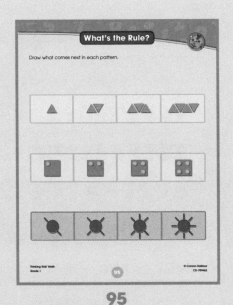

Puppy Patterns

Name each pattern using letters. Then, use counters to copy the pattern.

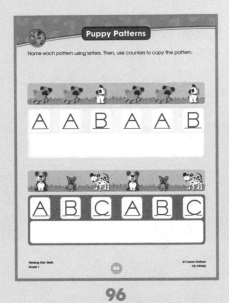

A A B A A B

A B C A B C

What Comes Next?

Draw the shape that comes next in each pattern. Tell whether the shape was slid, turned, or flipped.

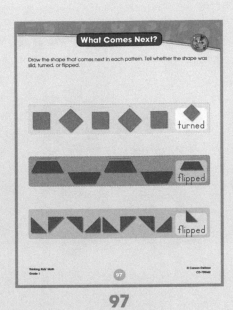

turned

flipped

flipped

Bead a Pattern

Put counters on the blank beads to continue each pattern.

Going Up!

Finish each pattern.

1 2 3 4 5 6 7 8

0 2 4 6 8 10 12 14

10 11 12 13 14 15 16 17

Going Up!

Finish each pattern.

1 3 5 7 9 11 13 15

5 6 7 8 9 10 11 12

11 12 13 14 15 16 17 18

Answer Key

101

102

103

104

105

106

Answer Key

Bubble, Bubble

Put the same color of counters on each pair of bubbles that have the same sum.

2+3 and 3+2   4+6 and 6+4
2+5 and 5+2   5+6 and 6+5
3+5 and 5+3   3+9 and 9+3
4+5 and 5+4   4+9 and 9+4

107

Seesaw Sums

Put counters on each side of the seesaw to test each equation. Circle the equations that are true. Cross out the equations that are not true.

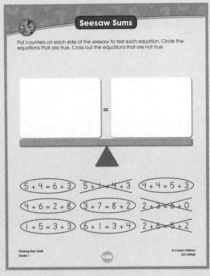

108

Tipping the Scales

Look at the numbers below each scale. Write >, <, or = to compare each set of numbers.

> greater than   **<** less than   **=** equal to

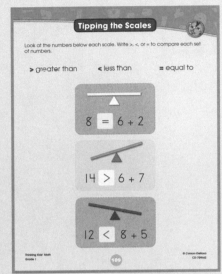

$8 = 6 + 2$

$14 > 6 + 7$

$12 < 8 + 5$

109

Tipping the Scales

Look at the numbers below each scale. Write >, <, or = to compare each set of numbers.

> greater than   **<** less than   **=** equal to

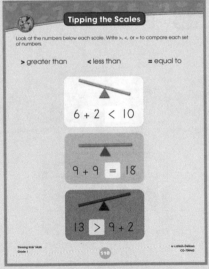

$6 + 2 < 10$

$9 + 9 = 18$

$13 > 9 + 2$

110

Name That Figure!

Circle the word that describes each object.

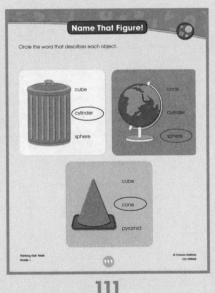

111

Name That Figure!

Circle the word that describes each object.

112

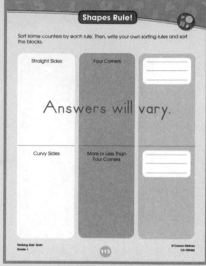

113

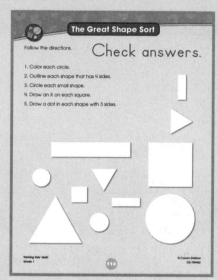

114

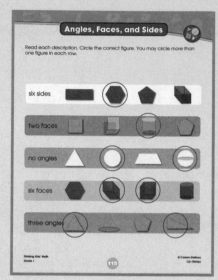

115

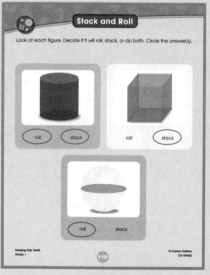

116

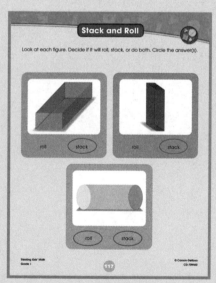

117

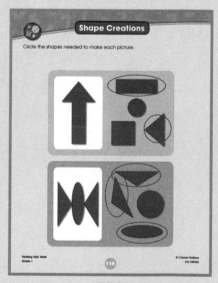

118

Shape Creations

Circle the shapes needed to make each picture.

119

Castle Shapes

Describe where each shape is using color words, shape names, and position words.

Answers will vary.

120

Beth's Beagle

Follow the directions to help Beth find her dog. Write the missing words in the directions as you go. Draw an X where she finds the dog.

Walk past 2 trees. Turn right and walk to the house.

Turn left and walk to the **rocks**.

Turn right and walk to the **pond**.
Turn right and walk past the pond.

Turn right and walk to the **garden**.
Turn left and walk to the end of the garden.
Turn left and walk straight to find the dog.

The dog is in the **doghouse**.

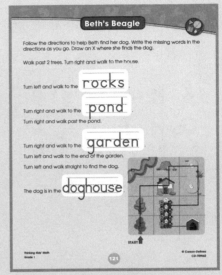

121

Where's the Bear?

Use numbers, letters, and shape names to describe where the bear is.

Answers will vary.

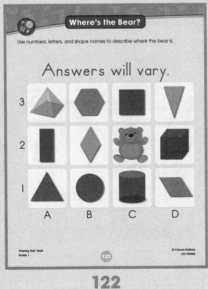

122

Flip, Slide, and Turn!

Place each block on its picture. Then, trace its flip, slide, and turn.

Shape	Flip	Slide	Turn

123

Simply Symmetrical

Circle the shapes and letters that have symmetry.

124

Alphabet Symmetry

Circle each letter of the alphabet that has symmetry. Draw Xs on the letters that do not have symmetry.

125

Flipping for Letters

Draw how each letter would look after a slide, a flip, and a turn.

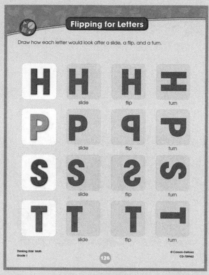

126

Find That Face!

Circle the shape of the bottom face of each figure.

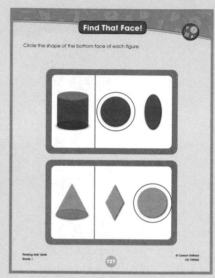

127

Find That Face!

Circle the shape of the bottom face of each figure.

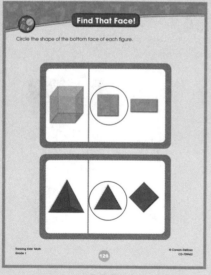

128

Picnic Perimeters

Write how many total steps it will take for each ant to walk around his picnic blanket.

129

Measure It!

How long is your desk? Measure it with each object. Write the numbers.

130

Answer Key

Will's Worms

Will found some worms in his backyard. Use two fingers at a time to measure each worm.

Answers will vary.

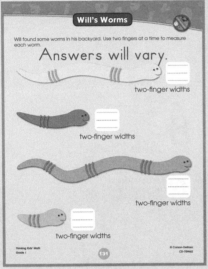

two-finger widths

two-finger widths

two-finger widths

two-finger widths

131

Pencils or Cubes?

Use unsharpened pencils to measure the length of each object. Then, use counters to measure the length of each object.

Answers will vary.

desk — about ____ pencils or about ____ counters

your arm — about ____ pencils or about ____ counters

book — about ____ pencils or about ____ counters

your shoe — about ____ pencils or about ____ counters

chair seat — about ____ pencils or about ____ counters

132

Animal Measures

Measure the animals in inches and centimeters. Write each measurement on the line.

5 inches

5 centimeters

133

Animal Measures

Measure the animals in inches and centimeters. Write each measurement on the line.

2 inches

4 centimeters

134

Know Your Units

Circle the unit of measurement that best measures each object.

car — inch (foot)

notebook — (inch) foot

dog — (inch) foot

shoe — (centimeter) meter

paper clip — (centimeter) meter

bee — (centimeter) meter

135

Biggest Blankets

Use counters to find the area (A) of each blanket.

Answers will vary.

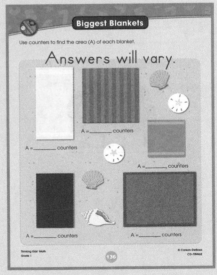

A = ____ counters

A = ____ counters

A = ____ counters

A = ____ counters

A = ____ counters

136

Answer Key

Measure Up!

Estimate the length of your desk. Then, measure your desk with each item.

Answers will vary.

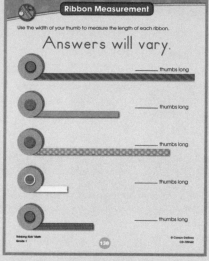

Estimate: _____ paper clips long

Actual: _____ paper clips long

Estimate: _____ pencils long

Actual: _____ pencils long

Estimate: _____ paintbrushes long

Actual: _____ paintbrushes long

Estimate: _____ scissors long

Actual: _____ scissors long

Thinking Kids' Math
Grade 1

137

© Carson-Dellosa
CD-704462

137

Ribbon Measurement

Use the width of your thumb to measure the length of each ribbon.

Answers will vary.

_____ thumbs long

_____ thumbs long

_____ thumbs long

_____ thumbs long

_____ thumbs long

Thinking Kids' Math
Grade 1

138

© Carson-Dellosa
CD-704462

138

Cube Counts

Measure the length of each object with counters. Write the measurement on the line.

Answers will vary.

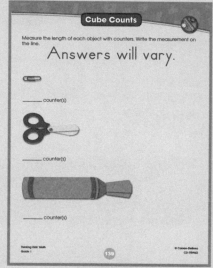

_____ counter(s)

_____ counter(s)

_____ counter(s)

Thinking Kids' Math
Grade 1

139

© Carson-Dellosa
CD-704462

139

Buggy About Measurement

Measure the length of each bug with paper clips. Write the measurement on the line.

Answers will vary.

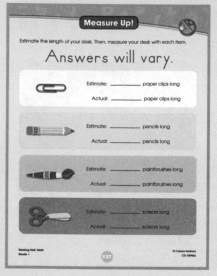

The ladybug is about _____ paper clips long.

The bee is about _____ paper clip long.

Thinking Kids' Math
Grade 1

140

© Carson-Dellosa
CD-704462

140

Order Up!

Number the events from 1 to 6 in the order in which they occur.

Eat breakfast.
2

Eat lunch.
4

Go to bed.
6

Go to school.
3

Woke up.
1

Eat dinner.
5

Thinking Kids' Math
Grade 1

141

© Carson-Dellosa
CD-704462

141

The Hands of Time

Draw the hands or write the numbers to show the time for each clock.

12:00

6:00

7:00

9:00

3:30

4:30

10:30

8:30

Thinking Kids' Math
Grade 1

142

© Carson-Dellosa
CD-704462

142

Answer Key

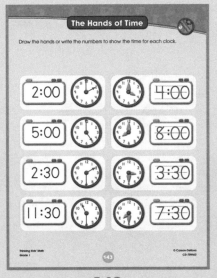

143

144

145

146

147

148

Answer Key

149

150

151

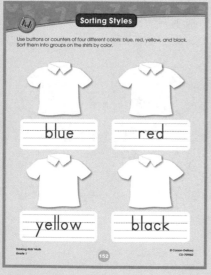

152

153

154

Answer Key

Shape Sorts

Put counters in each box that have something in common with the shape pictured.

Answers will vary.

155

A Colorful Graph

Sort a handful of counters by color. Put them in the correct rows.

Answers will vary.

red					
blue					
yellow					
green					
orange					

156

Pencil Poll Pictograph

Jon took a poll of four friends to see how many pencils each had in his or her pencil box. Use Jon's tally chart to draw the pencils in the graph.

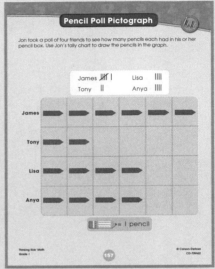

James 卌 I	Lisa 卌
Tony II	Anya 卌

= 1 pencil

157

Balloon Poll Pictograph

Jane took a poll of four friends to see how many balloons each had. Use Jane's tally chart to draw the balloons in the graph.

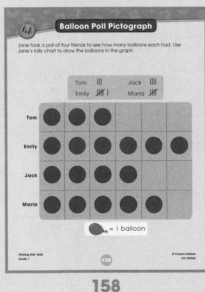

Tom III	Jack IIII
Emily 卌 I	Maria 卌

= 1 balloon

158

Backyard Bugs

Lin counted the bugs she collected in her backyard. Draw Xs in the spaces above each bug to make a bar graph of her data.

Backyard Bugs

159

Picnic Time

Brian counted the items at the picnic. Draw Xs in the spaces above each item to make a bar graph of his data.

Picnic Items

160

Answer Key

161 — Preferred Pets

Look at the results of a class survey about favorite pets. Draw smiley faces to show the data in a pictograph. Look at the key to see how many votes each smiley face stands for.

☺ = 2 votes

161

162 — Animal Graphs

Study the graph. Answer the questions.

Answers will vary.

What do the pictures show?
a. trees
b. animals
c. people

Write a title above the graph.

Write two facts from the graph.

162

163 — Sunny, Cloudy, or Rainy?

Mr. Kent's class kept track of the daily weather on the calendar last month. Use the calendar to answer the questions.

April

How many days were rainy? **3**

How many days were cloudy but not rainy? **6**

How many days were sunny? **14**

How many days are in the month? **30**

163

164 — Likely or Unlikely?

Circle likely or unlikely to answer each question.

If you were playing a game with this spinner, is it **likely** or **unlikely** that you would spin red?

likely   (unlikely)

If you picked a marble out of this bag without looking, is it **likely** or **unlikely** that you would pick a red one?

(likely)   unlikely

164

165 — Wishing Well

Decide how likely it is that a tossed coin will land on each well. Below each well, write more likely, likely, or less likely.

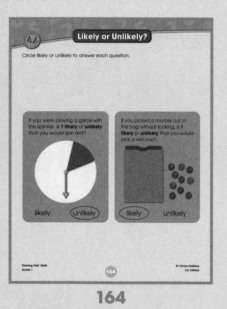

more likely

likely

less likely

165